PHOTOGRAPHY IN CONTEMPORARY GERMAN ART:

1960 TO THE PRESENT

PHOTOGRAPHY IN CONTEMPORARY GERMAN ART: 1960 TO THE PRESENT

GARY GARRELS

WALKER ART CENTER
MINNEAPOLIS

FIRST EDITION

Published in the United States of America by the Walker Art Center, Minneapolis, Minnesota.

Library of Congress Catalog Card Number: 91–51194
ISBN: 0–935640–37–1

Designer: Laurie Haycock Makela
Copy Editor: Phil Freshman
This book was typeset by Eric Malenfant on a Macintosh II with Quark Express using Franklin Gothic type (heads) and Bodoni (text). It was printed on Mohawk Superfine paper by Bolger Publications, Minneapolis.

PHOTOGRAPHY IN CONTEMPORARY GERMAN ART: 1960 TO THE PRESENT

WALKER ART CENTER
MINNEAPOLIS, MINNESOTA
FEBRUARY 9 – MAY 31, 1992

DALLAS MUSEUM OF ART
DALLAS, TEXAS
AND
MODERN ART MUSEUM OF FORT WORTH
FORT WORTH, TEXAS
AUGUST 16 – OCTOBER 11, 1992

GUGGENHEIM MUSEUM SOHO
NEW YORK, NEW YORK
DECEMBER 1992 – FEBRUARY 1993

PHOTOGRAPHY IN CONTEMPORARY GERMAN ART: 1960 TO THE PRESENT is made possible in part with funds provided by The Robert Mapplethorpe Foundation, Inc., New York, and in cooperation with the Goethe-Institut, Chicago.

This book is made possible in part by a grant from The Andrew W. Mellon Foundation in support of Walker Art Center publications.

Cover illustration:
Joseph Beuys
Iphigenia / Titus Andronicus 1985
photographic negatives with paint between glass plates in iron frame
28 x 21 5/8 in.
Courtesy Matthew Marks Gallery, New York

CONTENTS

In the course of organizing this exhibition, I have called upon many colleagues for information and consultation. Their time, thoughts, and knowledge have been crucial at several turns. Among them, I must especially thank: Bernhard Bürgi, Kunsthalle, Zurich; Susanne Ghez, The Renaissance Society at the University of Chicago; F. C. Gundlach, Hamburg; Ydessa Hendeles, Ydessa Hendeles Art Foundation, Toronto; Kaspar Koenig and Ulrich Wilmes, Portikus, Frankfurt; Mario Kramer, Museum für Moderne Kunst, Frankfurt; Ulrich Luckhardt, Hamburger Kunsthalle; Jochen Poetter, Kunsthalle Baden-Baden; Lothar Schirmer, Schirmer/Mosel Verlag, Munich; Ann Temkin, Philadelphia Museum of Art; and Charles Wright, Dia Center for the Arts, New York.

In addition to the lenders to the exhibition, a number of galleries and individuals supplied vital photographs, study materials, and loan assistance. These include: Susan Dunne, Pace Gallery, New York; Richard Flood and Barbara Gladstone, Barbara Gladstone Gallery, New York; David Nolan, David Nolan Gallery, New York; Lisa Spellman, 303 Gallery, New York; Helen van der Meij, London; Ealan Wingate, New York; and Wolfgang Wittrock, Düsseldorf.

Individuals working at galleries and with artists represented in the exhibition responded enthusiastically and expeditiously to my many queries. In this connection, it was my good fortune to work with: Sean Caley Regen and Jib Polhemus, Stuart Regen Gallery, Los Angeles; Claudia Carsons, Luhring Augustine Gallery, New York; Brigitte Junker, Bernd and Anna Blume studio, Cologne; Susanne Kleine, Galerie Max Hetzler, Cologne; Priamo Lozada, Jeannie Freilich, and Jill Sussman, Marian Goodman Gallery, New York; Angelika Thill, Gerhard Richter studio, Cologne; Mia von Sadovszky and Melissa Chappell, Luhring Augustine Hetzler Gallery, Los Angeles; Meg Malloy, Edition Schellmann, New York; and Pascale Zoller, Galerie Beyeler, Basel.

I have had numerous discussions with colleagues who will present papers at the February 1992 symposium *Photography in Contemporary German Art*, co-organized by the Walker Art Center and the Department of Art History, University of Minnesota. While their own contributions will be forthcoming at the symposium and included in the book of essays to be based on it, our conversations have been very helpful in clarifying many of my thoughts on the subject. At this early point, I must thank: Rosemarie Haag Bletter, New York; Benjamin H. D. Buchloh, New York; Jean-François Chevrier, Paris; Hans Dickel, Berlin; Charles W. Haxthausen, Minneapolis; Martin Hentschel, Frankfurt; Ulrich Loock, Bern; Christopher Phillips, New York; and Eric L. Santner, Princeton, New Jersey. In connection with the symposium, I am especially grateful to Charles Haxthausen, Associate Professor, Department of Art History, University of Minnesota for his dialogue and support.

This large and complicated project — which includes the exhibition, publications, and symposium — has been organized in an extremely short period of time. The early and enthusiastic response I received from colleagues at museums in the United States that will also present this exhibition was immensely heartening. It has been a pleasure and privilege to work with Annegreth Nill, Curator of Contemporary Art, Dallas Museum of Art; Jim Fisher, Curator, Modern Art Museum of Fort Worth; Michael Goven, Deputy Director, Guggenheim Museum, New York; and most especially with Nancy Spector, Associate Curator for Research, Guggenheim Museum.

Having arrived at the Walker only last May, I discovered with extreme happiness and pride a peerless group of professionals. Among them I must especially thank Gwen Bitz, Registrar; Cameron Zebrun, Manager, Program Services; Laurie Haycock Makela, Senior Graphic Designer; Phil Freshman, Editor; Mary Polta, Finance Director; David M. Galligan, Administrative Director; Toby Kamps, Curatorial/ Education Intern; and Henrietta Dwyer, my assistant and secretary. I count the museum's other visual arts curators — Elizabeth Armstrong, Peter Boswell, and Joan Rothfuss — as both colleagues and friends, and I thank them for their support.

The subject of this exhibition and book is one that has been at the center of many conversations over the years between Walker Art Center director Kathy Halbreich and myself. It is a special pleasure to be working with her and to be sharing her intellectual commitment and resourcefulness in the realization of this, my first project at the museum.

My thanks go as well to the rest of the Walker staff. They have welcomed me warmly and have given unstintingly of their skills, energy, and friendship. They are a remarkable group, and I am fortunate to be working with them. In a parallel fashion, the trustees of the Walker have shared their commitment to this institution with me. Their support and trust have been invaluable in pushing this project forward.

No matter how much thought and effort are brought to such a project, it cannot be realized without substantial financial support. The Robert Mapplethorpe Foundation in New York, through its board of trustees and with the enthusiasm of Michael Stout and Tina Summerlin, generously provided funds. The cooperation of the Goethe-Institut, Chicago, through Dr. Hans-Georg Knopp and Angela Greiner, also has been important in realizing this project.

My greatest gratitude goes to the artists in this exhibition who, without exception, have given generously of their time, their thoughts, and their work. In many cases, they have helped facilitate loans or have lent work from their own studios or collections. Involvement with them and their work has only strengthened my regard and respect for their achievements. I hope my efforts in presenting their art to a broader public parallels in some modest way their intelligence and spirit.

Finally, my heartfelt thanks go to Richard Hoblock for listening and reading and believing in the merits of this project.

GARY GARRELS

SENIOR CURATOR

JANUARY 1992

LENDERS TO THE EXHIBITION

A checklist for the exhibition is not included in this publication but is available upon request. There will be some changes in presentation at each museum to which the exhibition travels, though a core grouping will remain consistent. Lenders to the exhibition have thus been extraordinarily gracious and generous in sharing their works for the course of this exhibition. I am extremely grateful to the following museums, galleries, and individuals for their cooperation and loans:

Jürgen Becker, Galerie Jürgen Becker, Hamburg
Ernst Beyeler, Galerie Beyeler, Basel
Dr. Ernst Busche, Busche Galerie, Cologne
Elaine and Werner Dannheisser, New York
Sammlung Claus and Sylvia Schröder, Hamburg
Ellyn and Saul Dennison, Bernardsville, New Jersey
Collection Dürckheim, Family Trust, Entraching, Germany
Suzanne and Howard Feldman, New York
Helyn and Ralph Goldenberg, Chicago
Marian Goodman, Marian Goodman Gallery, New York
Christoph von Hardenberg, Hamburg
Collection Edward and Betty Harris, Chicago
The Heithoff Family Collection, Minneapolis
Max Hetzler, Galerie Max Hetzler, Cologne
Jörg Johnen, Galerie Johnen & Schöttle, Cologne
Phillip Johnstone, Director, and the Trustees, The Carnegie Museum of Art, Pittsburgh
Patricia Kahane, Vienna
Volker Koch, Nuremberg
Uli Knecht, Stuttgart
Sabine Knust, Galerie Sabine Knust, Munich
Hans-Peter Labin, Hamburg
Ronald Lauder, New York
Roland Augustine and Lawrence Luhring, Luhring Augustine Gallery, New York
Luhring Augustine Hetzler Gallery, Los Angeles
Linda and Harry Macklowe, New York
Paul Maenz, Cologne
Matthew Marks, Matthew Marks Gallery, New York
Evan Maurer, Director; Richard Campbell, Curator of Prints and Drawings; and the Trustees, The Minneapolis Institute of Arts
Kunsthalle Nürnberg
Produzentengalerie, Hamburg
Stuart Regen, Stuart Regen Gallery, Los Angeles
Jörg Schellmann, Edition Schellman, Munich
Wilhelm Schurmann, Herzogenrath, Germany
Ileanna Sonnabend and Antonio Homem, Sonnabend Gallery, New York
Gerd de Vries, Cologne
Mike and Penny Winton, Minneapolis

FOREWORD

This exhibition, spanning three decades of investigation into the shifting meaning and properties of the photographic medium, is the first organized by Gary Garrels since he assumed the post of senior curator at the Walker in May 1991. While he and I had discussed the subject at hand many times during the past few years, Gary's ability to organize on such short notice an exhibition of this ambition and perspicacity is testimony to his extraordinary powers of concentration as well as to his command of the field. His talents were magnified by those of the many Walker staff members who helped him realize the exhibition, the two accompanying publications, and the international symposium, which brings together scholars — primarily emerging ones — from France, Germany, and the United States.

I also am especially grateful to the artists, all of whom lent early, generous, and crucial support; they enthusiastically discussed with Gary the grouping of work to be included and the architectural frame within which it might be best highlighted. While I like to think the Walker is particularly fleet of foot — able to react quickly to the demands of both curators and artists — my directorial colleagues were equally adept, swiftly agreeing to juggle their exhibition schedules in order to accommodate ours. Richard Brettell, director of the Dallas Museum of Art; Marla Price, director of the Modern Art Museum of Fort Worth; and Thomas Krens, director of the Guggenheim Museum, agreed to host this exhibition, and I am extremely appreciative of their support.

It is my expectation that this exhibition will shed new light on the synthesizing powers of the nineteen German artists represented. It certainly will help all of us recognize the generative role photography has played in the accomplishments of these artists, many of whom have been known simply, and somewhat simplistically, as either painters or photographers.

KATHY HALBREICH

DIRECTOR

PHOTOGRAPHY IN CONTEMPORARY GERMAN ART: 1960 TO THE PRESENT

GARY GARRELS

INTRODUCTION

German artists in the last thirty years have made ambitious use of photography, producing works that equal the widely acknowledged German achievements of the same period in painting and sculpture. Yet the critical, generative role the photographic medium has played in contemporary German art remains relatively unrecognized. This exhibition has been conceived as a framework for understanding the importance that the photographic medium has had for contemporary German artists and as an introduction to some of the distinguished work produced since 1960 using photography.

Beginning in the late 1950s, artists throughout the world began making work that disrupted distinctions between traditional media — painting, sculpture, drawing, printmaking, and photography. The old labels of painter, sculptor, and photographer often were challenged, as artists moved between various media or combined media into hybrid and synthesized forms. New media involving real time, such as video and performance art, began to be incorporated into artists' activity, as did film, which previously, with only a handful of exceptions, had been on the periphery of the visual arts. While there had been precedents for these experiments among some artists in the 1920s and 1930s, World War II disrupted and brought to a halt much of this activity. Not until the late 1950s and the early 1960s, with the expansion of the postwar economy, the proliferation of international travel and communication, and the explosion of the mass media, were conditions ripe for a full-scale resurgence of nontraditional activity by visual artists.[1]

Under these new conditions, artists began using photography in ways conceptually and materially different from those generally practiced prior to 1960, in which the emphasis had been on making fine photographic prints in limited multiple editions. Traditional practices, while not abandoned, were now radically expanded upon by a wide range of artists. Unique works, images combining mechanical and handworked processes, photographic prints combined with other materials, and explosions of scale changed equally the processes of making photographs and the images that resulted. Increasingly, artists also began reexamining commercial production technologies, uses of photographic images, and traditional considerations of placement of image on the page, in relation to objects, or in a room. The photographic medium came to be recognized as having enormous physical and conceptual capacities that could touch on and expand the potential of other media as well. Thus relationships between photography and painting, photography and sculpture, photography and architecture, photography and film, and photography and mass-produced mechanical images all came to be explored as points along the continuum of the photographic medium.

While not unique in their development of the potential of photography, German artists have been at the forefront in the integration and expansion of the medium in contemporary art. Germany has a long history of intensive involvement with photography, including its technical, social, and aesthetic aspects. Links with the past and with particular precedents of photography have been important in setting the stage for the achievements of contemporary artists. The extraordinary explorations of the photographic medium made in Germany between the world wars, roughly from 1919 to 1939, continue to have an impact on most of the contemporary German artists using photography.[2] The diverse range of work produced in those two decades included straightforward image-making, unusual perspectives, and visual effects from the unique properties of cameras and film, and the manipulation of film and photochemical processes to create abstract and expressive images. All of these practices have been reengaged by contemporary artists as they have pushed photography into new territories.

Also of significance have been the presence and accomplishments of artists who established themselves in the early 1960s as key figures in contemporary German art — most importantly Joseph Beuys and the team of Bernd and Hilla Becher. Both Beuys and Bernd Becher taught at the Kunstakademie (art academy) in Düsseldorf, one of the most prominent schools for artists in Germany, and their influence on subsequent generations of artists has been immense. Their attitudes toward the photographic medium could not have been more different, but both were committed to intense involvement with their students and led them in the most rigorous and challenging ways. Beuys' influence was particularly important on the generation that emerged in the 1970s, while the Bechers' impact has been most evident among young artists whose work matured in the 1980s.[3]

In organizing this exhibition the choice was made not to attempt an inclusive and didactic survey representative of all trends, movements, groups, and schools. Artists working in East Germany prior to the reunification of the country in 1990 are not considered here, since artistic conditions there were completely separate from those in West Germany. Also, photographers who use the medium only in traditional pictorial or documentary ways have not been included. Many of the artists represented here are concerned, however, with these means of expression and do produce carefully composed and printed images. All of the artists were chosen because of the importance and strength of their photographic works and for the ways in which they have expanded the material and conceptual boundaries of the medium. Nineteen artists are included in the exhibition, representing work produced over three decades. Single bodies of work or focused groupings have been selected that are among each artist's most distinguished efforts and that convey as fully as possible an appreciation of that artist's vision and the issues and practices underlying his or her work. In most cases, the images have been chosen in close cooperation with the artists or with their assistance in developing and, in some cases, executing the presentation of the work.

While the exhibition focuses on individual artists, some overall tendencies can be noted. In the 1960s and early 1970s artists often used photographs in ways consistent with the practices of Minimalism and Conceptual Art. For example, they explored the possibilities of series as permutations within a general system and often presented their series in gridded formats. Issues of Pop Art, in which images from the mass media are fetishized and transformed or re-presented, were common concerns. The prevalent technologies made color photographs rare and single prints of modest size common. Artistically — and generally — the 1970s were not marked by a dominant attitude. In the photography of that decade approaches first developed in the 1960s were continued and consolidated. Characteristic of the latter decade, too, was a preoccupation with psychology, seen in an emphasis on introspection and individual expression. In the 1980s a clearer and more coherent vision arose. Careful craft, large formats, and the dominance of color were the most visible responses to the new and highly accessible technological means of those years. But these developments were also a response to the return to traditional object-making and the salience of painting at the beginning of the decade. While artists often systematically explored subjects in series, the photographs they produced are singular objects, either unique or printed in small editions. The 1980s also saw artists grappling again with issues that had emerged in the 1960s, including the role of the museum in exhibiting and interpreting art and the influence of popular culture on artists; in this way, the work of the three decades under consideration comes full circle. What is clear throughout, of course, is that work in the photographic medium parallels or extends the attitudes and practices prevalent in other media.

A subtext of much of this work done from the 1960s to the present is a reckoning with German history, specifically with the Nazi period and the circumstances surrounding World War II. In various ways, artists of the last thirty years have endeavored to penetrate this history in order to reclaim German culture from the ashes of the Nazi tragedy and to express attitudes alternative to Nazi ideology. At the same time, German photographers typically have sought to celebrate contemporary internationalism and to find a common ground with other artists of the industrialized West. In particular, German artists have engaged in a highly complex and vital dialogue with artists in the United States. For artists in both countries photography has been a crucial medium, and so it must figure centrally in any understanding of the art that has been made in the West since 1960.

This book includes entries that have been written to provide both historical background on and interpretive keys to the work of each of the artists represented. The entries have been arranged in a loosely chronological order corresponding to the decade in which each artist first emerged; this arrangement, in turn, follows as closely as possible the floor plan of the associated exhibition. Entries focus on the pieces presented in the exhibition but in the context of each artist's overall development and work. Summary bibliographic references on each of the artists and on the subject of photography in contemporary German art as a whole also have been provided. While the entries and this publication have been prepared for a general public, a companion volume of essays, drawn from the symposium presented in conjunction with the Minneapolis presentation of the exhibition, will contain more exhaustive and scholarly examinations of the artists' work and of a wide range of topics relevant to serious consideration of the subject that can only be touched on here.

In short, this exhibition and book are intended as an introduction to the subject, not as a comprehensive summary. The attempt has been made to join historical objectivity with personal judgment and response. The hope in organizing the exhibition has been to inspire further consideration of each of the artists included here and of the crucial position of photography in contemporary German art.

1 See Barbara Haskell, *Blam!: The Explosion of Pop, Minimalism, and Performance, 1958 – 1964*, exh. cat. (New York: Whitney Museum of American Art in association with W. W. Norton and Company, 1984); *'60/'80: Attitudes/Concepts/Images*, exh. cat. (Amsterdam: Stedelijk Museum, 1982); and *Breakthroughs: Avant-Garde Artists in Europe and America, 1950 – 1990*, exh. cat. (New York: Rizzoli International Publications in association with Wexner Center for the Arts, Ohio State University, Columbus, 1991).

2 See Van Deren Coke, *Avant-Garde Photography in Germany, 1919 – 1939* (New York: Pantheon, 1982); and Maria Morris Hambourg and Christopher Phillips, *The New Vision: Photography between the World Wars*, exh. cat. (New York: Metropolitan Museum of Art, 1989).

3 For an examination of Beuys' influence, see Stephan von Wiese, *Brennpunkt Düsseldorf-Joseph Beuys — Die Akademie — Der allgemeine Aufbruch*, exh. cat. (Kunstmuseum Düsseldorf, 1987) (German). For an examination of the influence of Bernd and Hilla Becher, see *Aus der Distanz: Photographien von Bernd und Hilla Becher, Andreas Gursky, Candida Höfer, Axel Hütte, Thomas Ruff, Thomas Struth, Petra Wunderlich*, exh. cat. (Düsseldorf: Kunstsammlung Nordrhein-Westfalen, 1991) (German).

JOSEPH BEUYS

Joseph Beuys stands out now, six years after his death, as the most important European artist of the postwar era. From the time he was appointed professor at the art academy in Düsseldorf in 1961 until he died in 1986, he exerted a profound influence on contemporary art, both through his own art and through his impact on other artists and his students. He considered his teaching both within and outside the academy to be integral to his artistic activity. In 1967 he founded the German Student Party, an association of students at the academy. In 1972, for *documenta 5*, the large international art exhibition in Kassel, he opened an office for his Organization for Direct Democracy, from which he engaged in public debate on democracy and art for the 100-day duration of the exhibition. After that, with the writer Heinrich Böll, he established the Free International University for Creativity and Interdisciplinary Research (FIU). Many of the leading figures in contemporary German art studied with Beuys, including, in this exhibition, Lothar Baumgarten, Bernhard Blume, Anselm Kiefer, Imi Knoebel, and Katharina Sieverding.

Beuys' aim was radical: to expand the potential of art and human creativity. To help achieve this goal, he sought to eliminate constrictive boundaries and definitions concerning the nature of art and the role of the artist. His work spreads across a continuum, including traditional sculptural objects, installations of elaborate arrangements of various materials in rooms, performances, collections of materials and remnants from these performances, and thousands of drawings. With his performances, Beuys attempted to collapse the boundaries between art and life, between process and the static object. In a 1970 interview he stated: "The sentence 'Everybody is an artist' simply means to point out that the human being is a creative being, that he is a creator, and what's more, that he can be productive in a great many different ways. To me, it's irrelevant whether a product comes from a painter, from a sculptor or from a physicist."[1]

Beuys was a pioneer in producing a variety of objects called multiples, which were a continuation of the tradition of printmaking — but not limited to works on paper — in which works are made in small and sometimes very large editions. He used the multiple as a means by which to develop his ideas and expand the public that those ideas would reach. Photographic images were integral to his concept of multiples, and they occupied an important position among the potential materials for his art. As Jörg Schellmann, editor of the catalogue raisonné of Beuys' multiples, has written: "Beuys' production of editions differs from that of other artists in that it does not simply consist of printed graphics and multiple objects, but includes objects, objects-prints, prints, publications, leaflets, postcards, photos, printed matter, records, audio cassettes, video tapes, films, etc., and many combinations of these media. It is fundamental to Beuys' work and to his 'extended concept of art' that his production eludes division into compartmentalized art historical definitions."[2]

Beuys had a deep and abiding interest in science, and his attitude toward art as a means of making visible the invisible, of making known the unknown, found a parallel in science and in photography. The chemical processes involved in making the photographic print, the transfer of image through light onto a gelatin film, and the origins of photography in science all were important to him. Photographs were invented in two forms in 1839: the daguerreotype, devised by the French artist Louis-Jacques-Mandé Daguerre; and the calotype, invented by the English amateur scientist William Henry Fox Talbot. Beuys saw himself as carrying on the tradition of fusing science and art. He also recognized the versatility of the photograph as both record and interpretative document, as having its own physical and material qualities, and as having the capacity for replicability and thereby dispersion to a wide audience.

A tireless teacher and traveler, Beuys generally worked accompanied by a photographer, or on occasion a filmmaker, who would take images from his lectures and performances. Beuys often edited, sometimes altered, and then presented these photographic images in various ways, on occasion incorporated with other objects. One of his well-known performances was entitled *Celtic*, which he first presented in 1970 in Edinburgh and, with variations, in 1971 in Basel. It is from the second performance that the images for one of the multiples included in this exhibition were made.

A performance of *Celtic* can briefly be described as follows: Beuys would stand still for some forty minutes while music — a piano being tuned — by the Danish avant-garde composer Henning Christiansen was played. Beuys then would scribble on a portable blackboard and push it around on the floor for an equal length of time. Films of events by Beuys would be shown. Then, for more than an hour and a half, he would scrape bits of gelatin off the walls, put them on a tray, and empty the tray over his head in a convulsive movement. After dumping the gelatin, he "raised the blackboard, which bore a scene from the Grail legend, above his head, uttered unintelligible noises, and for more than half an hour stood, spear in hand, behind the board as it lay on the floor: Beuys, guardian of the Holy Grail. Then he strapped a flashlight to each of his thighs and stepped into a tub of water; his partner, Christiansen, poured a can of water over his head."[3] His colleague Caroline Tisdall has written of this performance that Beuys created "an ambiguous mixture of pagan and Christian symbolism, combining suggestions of purification and therapy with arcane references to the Age of Aquarius and alchemical principles."[4]

For this multiple, Beuys selected ten photographs of the performance, joining them with related objects — a film in a canister and a bottle sealed with beeswax. For other performances, he would sometimes choose a smaller number of images to include in a multiple or would use offset prints of the photographs that could be changed in scale or tone. In all cases, the images form a record, an interpretation, a means of sustaining interest in the ephemeral event and of reaching an audience that could not have seen the performance.

1 Joseph Beuys interview with Jörg Schellmann and Bernd Klüser in Jörg Schellmann, ed., *Joseph Beuys: Multiples*, 6th edn. (Munich and New York: Edition Schellmann, 1985), unpaginated (German, English).

2 Ibid. Editor's note.

3 Heiner Stachelhaus, *Joseph Beuys*, trans. David Britt (New York: Abbeville Press, 1991), p. 144. The description of this performance also is based on an account by Alastair Mackintosh quoted in Caroline Tisdall, *Joseph Beuys*, exh. cat. (New York: Solomon R. Guggenheim Museum, 1979), pp. 195 – 196.

4 Tisdall, p. 199.

Joseph Beuys *Celtic* + ∿∿∿ 1971

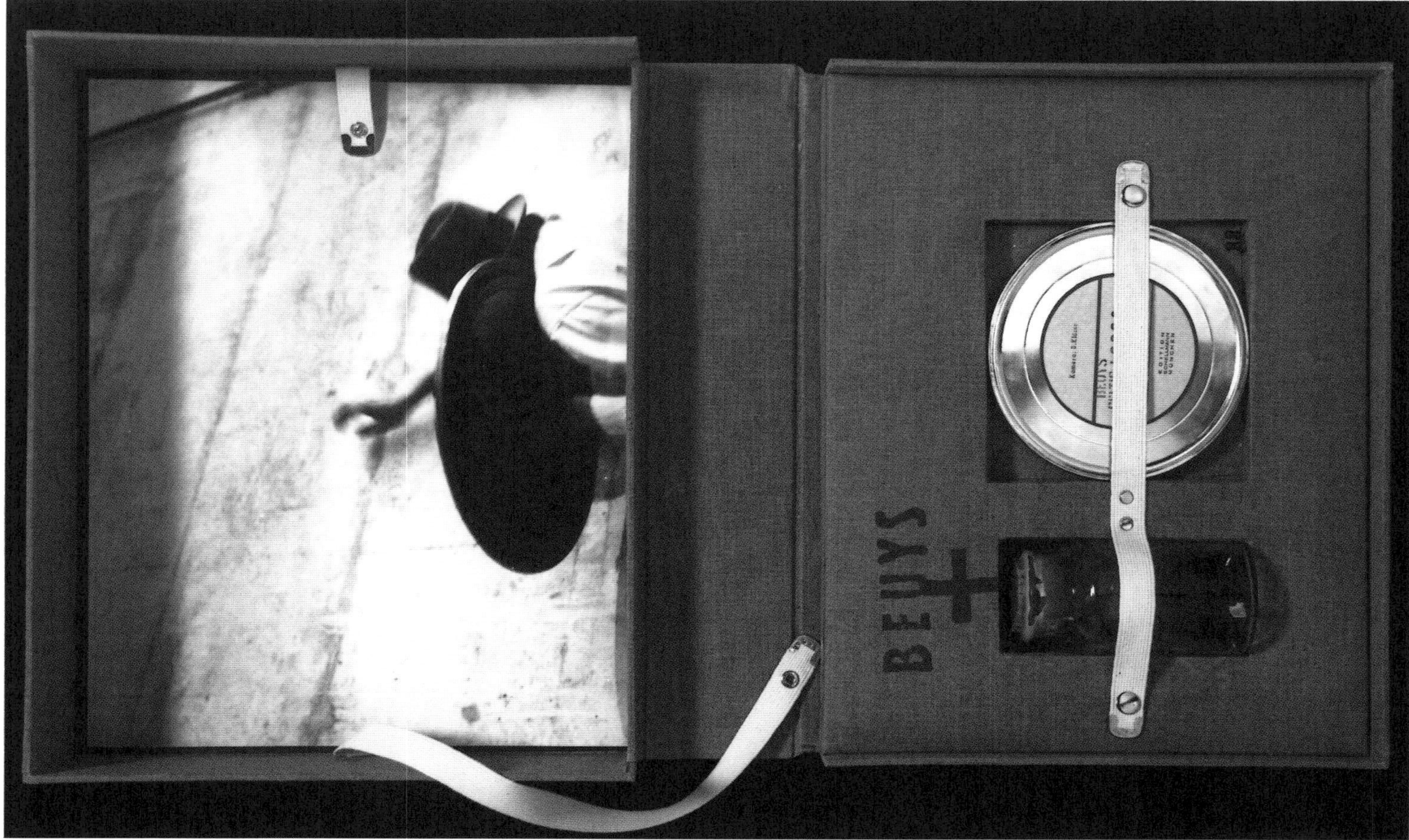

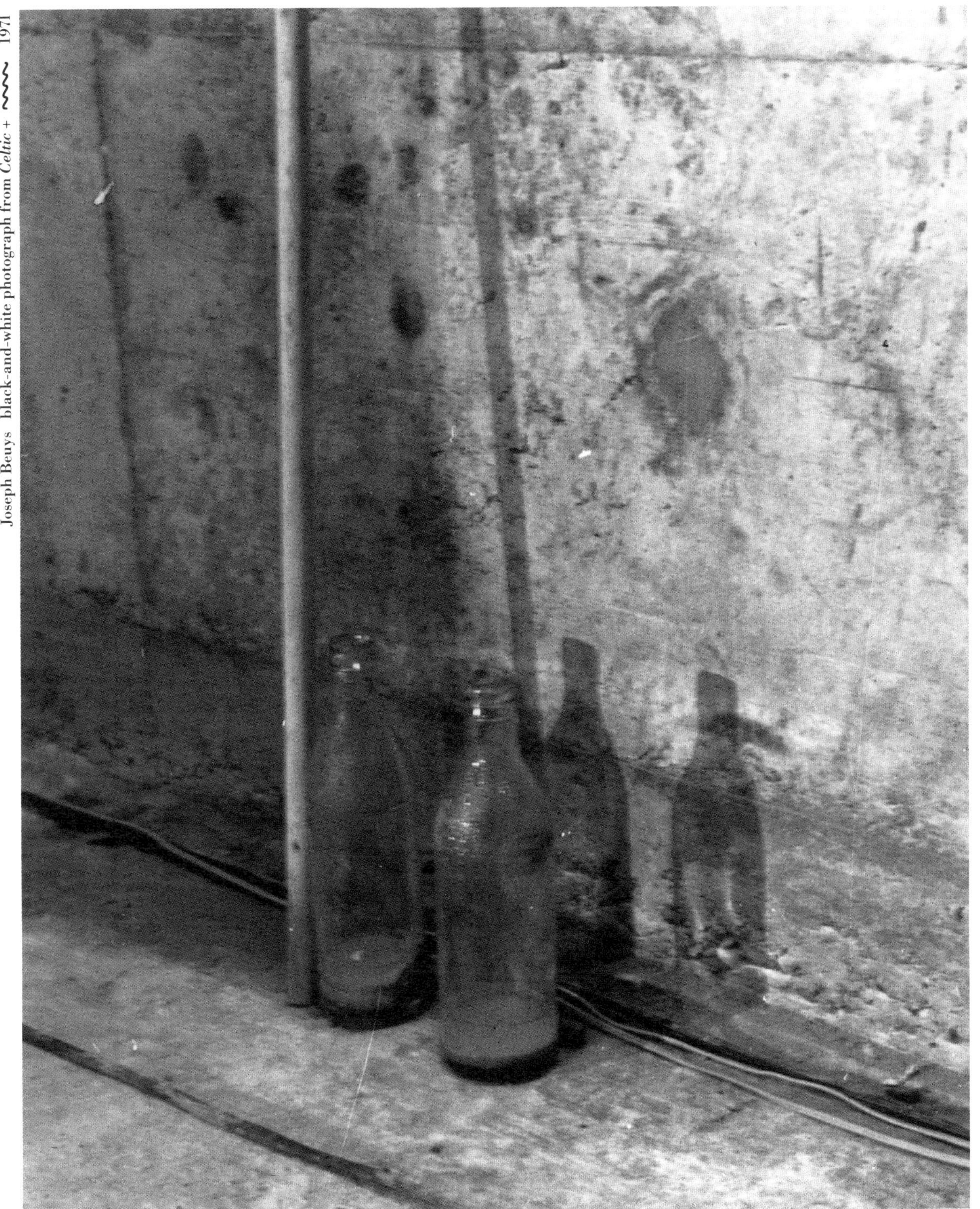

Joseph Beuys black-and-white photograph from *Celtic* + ~~~ 1971

Joseph Beuys black-and-white photograph from *Celtic* + 〰 1971

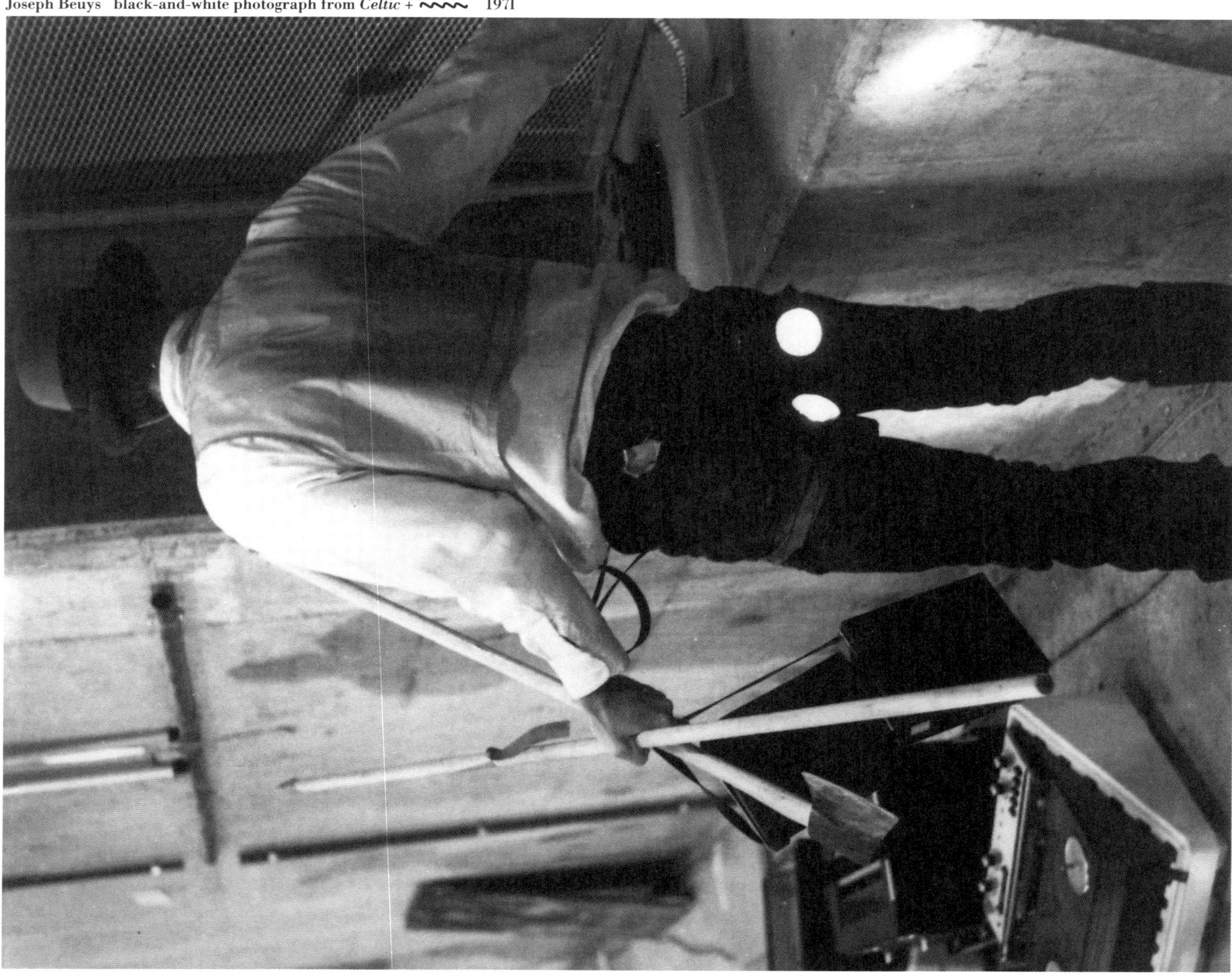

BERND AND HILLA BECHER

The husband-and-wife team of Bernd and Hilla Becher began collaborating in the late 1950s in Düsseldorf. They have lived and worked together since that time, traveling throughout Europe and the United States to make photographs of industrial structures — cooling towers, blast furnaces, mineheads, water towers, grain elevators, gas tanks, factory facades — and workers' housing. Their photographs are characterized by a singular, consistent style with a straight-on view, focus slightly above center, sharp detail, and overall lighting with little shadow. The frozen presence of their industrial subjects is devoid of human figures or operational activity. The Bechers revived and integrated important strands of photographic work developed in the 1920s and early 1930s, before the advent of the Nazi regime, by photographers such as Karl Blossfeldt, Albert Renger-Patzsch, and August Sander that were analytical and documentary but emphasized the formal qualities of the image and print. The Bechers' efforts to renew these traditions were made not only in appreciation of the work itself but also in reaction against the widespread emphasis on psychological content and romanticism in the visual arts after World War II and through the 1950s — exemplified in the United States by Abstract Expressionism and in Germany by the photographic movement known as Subjective Photography.

The Bechers' work first came to international attention in the late 1960s, presented and interpreted in the context of Minimal and Conceptual art, movements that shared with their work an emphasis on the roles of architectural space, social relations, straightforward materials, serial presentation, and an intellectually rigorous approach. Their first book, *Anonyme Skulpturen (Anonymous Sculpture)*, was published in 1970, and one of their first champions was the American Minimalist sculptor Carl Andre. Over the past twenty-five years the Bechers have exhibited their photographs in grids that they call "typologies." Each grouping is carefully composed of single views of similar structures seen from a consistent vantage point, and each emphasizes the distinctness of types and the individuality of structures within them. The result is a fascinating and powerful index to industrial-era structures. As many of these have, increasingly, become obsolete, the Bechers' ongoing project also serves as a catalogue of vanishing architecture. Since 1989 they occasionally have exhibited single prints shown in series. Either format — the typologies or the series — allows formal and didactic comparisons to be made. While they are best known for photographs that show entire large structures closely cropped in the frame of the image, they also have made series of details of structures as well as structures set within landscapes.

The Bechers take a fastidious approach to their craft, carrying out all phases of their work themselves: researching and finding their subjects, setting up and shooting the photographs, printing in the studio, and supervising every aspect of the production of their publications. Their work can be characterized as research into structural types, the taking of photographs and the formation of an archive of negatives, the printing of photographs for public exhibition, and the publication of books of single structural types. To date, they have completed five such books: *Framework Houses from the Siegen Industrial Area* (1977); *Fördertürme, Chevalments, Mineheads* (1985); *Water Towers* (1988); *Blast Furnaces* (1990); and, most recently, *Pennsylvania Coal Mine Tipples* (1991).

This exhibition includes the book and a large number of the prints from the Pennsylvania Coal Mine Tipple series. The tipples are one type of a structure called "mineheads," which are built over mines to bring the raw materials out of the ground. Tipples are unique to the United States and specific to eastern Pennsylvania. Families or partners build their own structures over shallow mines, sometimes abandoning them in difficult economic periods and rebuilding them later. Working in their usual manner, the Bechers took the coal mine tipple photographs over a period of years, in this case throughout the 1970s; groups of negatives were printed and exhibited on different occasions; and recently, a comprehensive set of photographs was made when the opportunity arose to produce the book.

In 1976 Bernd Becher was appointed professor at the art academy in Düsseldorf, introducing the study of photography there and establishing a central role for it among students. He and Hilla Becher have taught the students together and have had a far-reaching influence on many of them; a number are now highly regarded in their own right as photographer-artists. These include Thomas Ruff and Thomas Struth, whose work is presented in this exhibition, as well as Andreas Gursky, Candida Höfer, and Axel Hütte.

The Bechers' efforts can be seen as a sustained analytical inquiry into the nature of industrial society. Their work reveals how the formal properties of structures they photograph reflect functional operations but also how those properties reflect cultural practices. History is seen in these images as a mutable phenomenon, dependent upon changing economic imperatives and human desires. The Bechers' photographs, however, are not aloof or cold; often they are anthropomorphic — allowing us to identify with the individuality of various structures — and they convey the qualities of beauty, humor, and dignity.

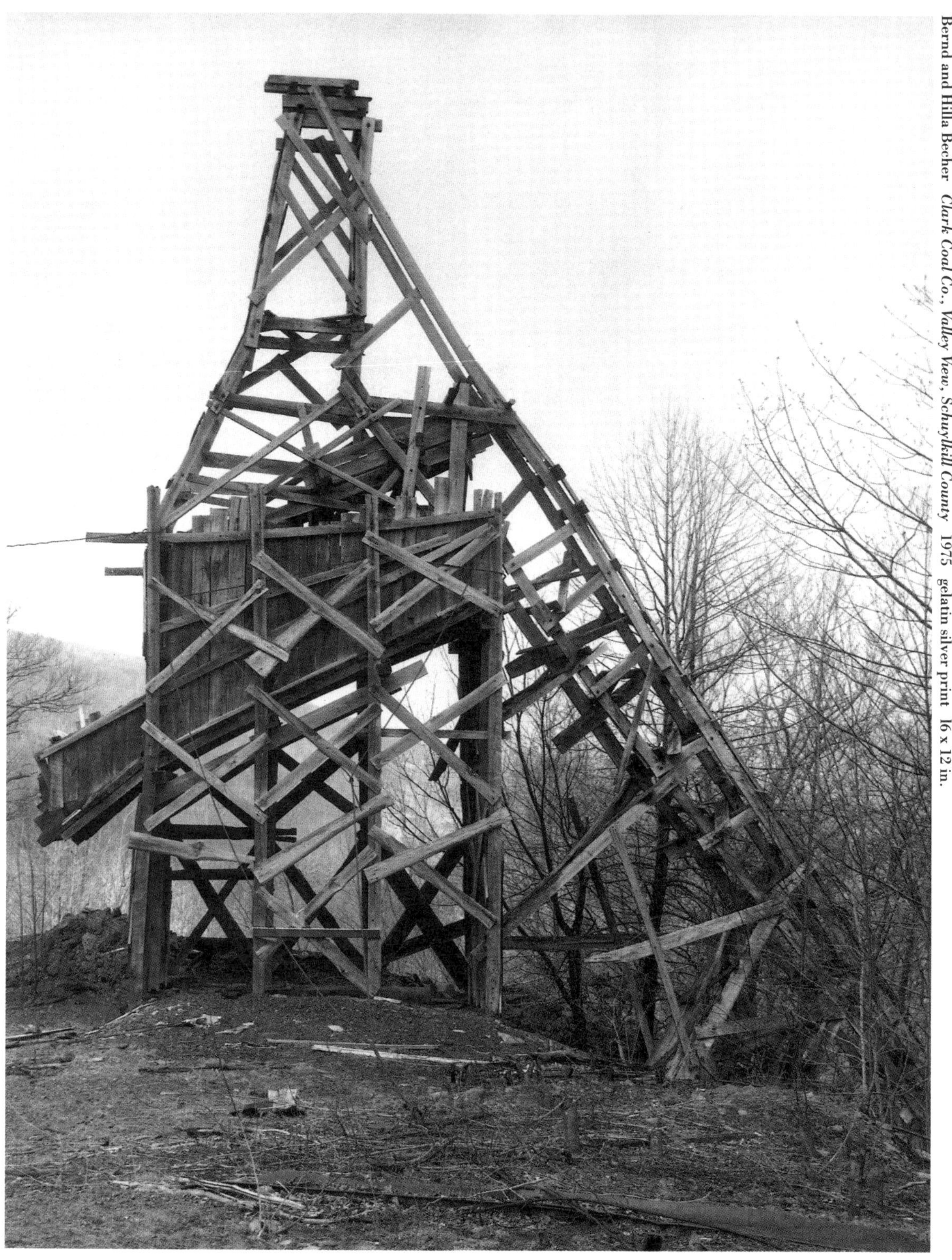

Bernd and Hilla Becher *Clark Coal Co., Valley View, Schuylkill County* 1975 gelatin silver print 16 x 12 in.

Bernd and Hilla Becher *Erdmann Brothers Coal Co., Valley View, Schuylkill County* 1974 gelatin silver print 16 x 12 in.

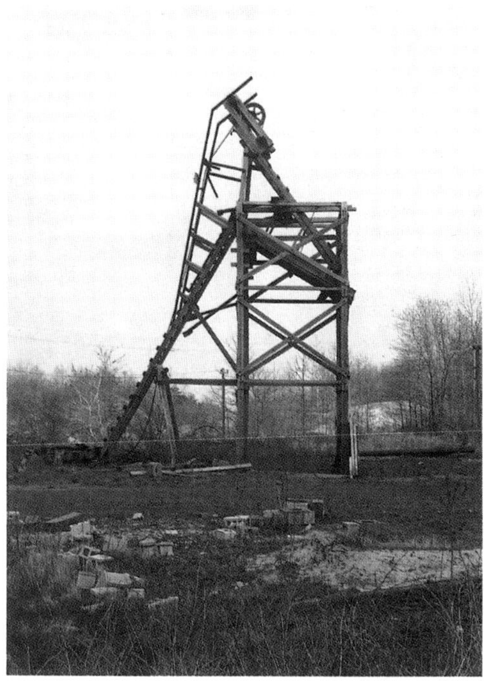

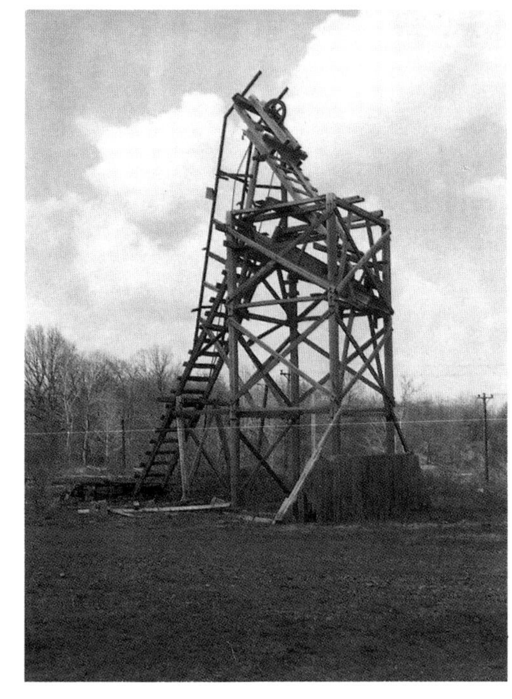

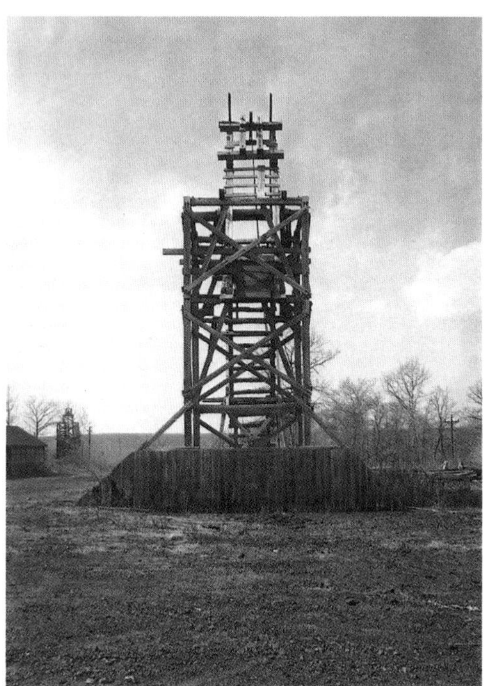

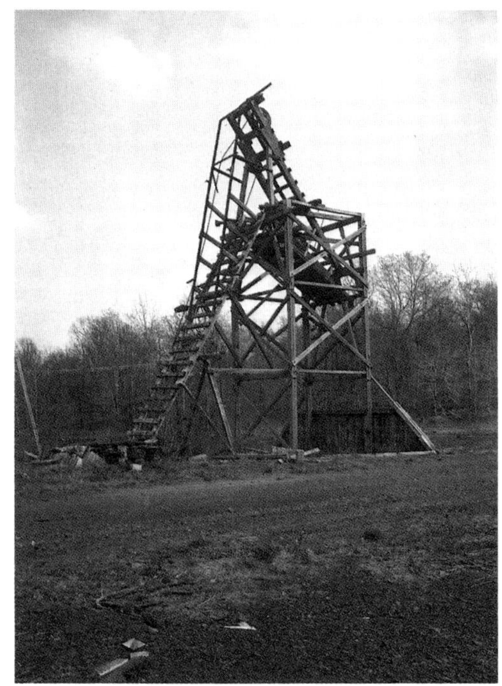

Bernd and Hilla Becher *Reed & Herb Coal Co., Joliette, Schuylkill County* 1975 four gelatin silver prints 4 x 4 in. each

GERHARD RICHTER

At the beginning of Gerhard Richter's career, in the early 1960s, the growth of mass media and the increasing profusion of images through photomechanical reproduction were phenomena that fascinated many artists — including Richard Artschwager, Roy Lichtenstein, Malcolm Morley, Sigmar Polke, and Andy Warhol. The traditions of culture represented by painting — the handworked, individually crafted object as a summation of an artist's knowledge and experience — seemed about to be overwhelmed by popular culture and the media age. The capabilities of the photograph to capture the immediacy and diversity of images of contemporary life appeared to be singular. The relationship between painting and photography was thrown open to a challenge that had not been raised in so fundamental a way since either the invention of photography in 1839 or the advent of the radical modernism formulated in the 1920s.

From his earliest works to his most recent ones, Richter has analyzed and expressed this uneasy relationship between painting and photography. He recognizes that both painting and photography share inadequacies in their abilities to render an image. Neither medium has the capacity for truth, he believes, but only partakes in the ever-shifting artistic conventions for examining the world. Richter's early paintings were of images based on photographs. In his later abstract canvases, the paint is treated like an emulsion, and an image is created that, although not representational, is filmic. A stylistic chameleon, he has aligned himself with neither figuration nor abstraction but has practiced both simultaneously. Richter consistently has been concerned with how pictures are made and the meanings that are associated with them. Pictures are autonomous for him, removed from reality, and therefore always bear some amount of distortion and some degree of abstraction. The reading of individual, and apparently personal gestures, which would seem to be the mark of painting, is given no more credit for its ability to reveal truth than is the image captured by the photograph. Both stand at a remove from experience; both could be called indexes to a common reality. Richter is interested in the variety of meeting points, the possibilities of shifting degrees of relationships between images and knowledge.

Richter is generally regarded as a painter, but this interpretation does not do him justice as an artist. A statement about his paintings that he made in 1972 in the catalogue accompanying his exhibition at the Venice Biennale remains crucial today: "It is not a question of imitating a photograph. I want to actually make a photograph. And because I want to go beyond the idea of photography conceived merely as a piece of light-sensitive paper, I make photographs with other means — not just pictures which are derived from photographs. The same holds true for pictures (abstracts, etc.) which, without a photographic model, produce photographs."[1]

One of Richter's great works is the compendium of photographic images, entitled *Atlas*, which he began making in 1962. It is an ongoing work in which he has collected found snapshots, images clipped from newspapers, photographs with sketches, and his own series of photographs. It was first exhibited in 1976 at the Museum Haus Lange in Krefeld, Germany, and then in expanded form in 1989 in Munich and in 1990 in Cologne. The images closely parallel, year by year, the subjects of Richter's paintings — figurative works, portraits, gestural abstractions, geometric abstractions, cityscapes and landscapes of forests, fields, sea, and sky, still-life studies, and studies for room installations. The final series of photographs to date relates to the Baader-Meinhof German terrorist group, active in the 1970s, which also was the subject of a widely exhibited series of Richter paintings from 1989. While it generally follows a chronological pattern and falls within thematic groupings, *Atlas* is a work without a precisely fixed order; the way it is shown depends upon the exhibition space in which it is sited. If shown in its entirety, it fills several rooms. For this exhibition, Richter has selected blocks of images that trace the range of subjects in the work as a whole. This presentation could be described as an index of an index, reinforcing as it does the characteristic removal and abstraction of Richter's work from a more complete reference outside itself. *Atlas* reveals the systematic but open-ended analysis central to his art; it bespeaks Richter's contained passion, his cool yet obsessive, skeptical but searching need to examine images and restructure them.

1 Quoted in Benjamin H. D. Buchloh, "Ready-made Photography and Painting in the Painting of Gerhard Richter," *Gerhard Richter: Abstract Paintings*, exh. cat. (Eindhoven: Stedelijk van Abbemuseum, 1978), p. 8.

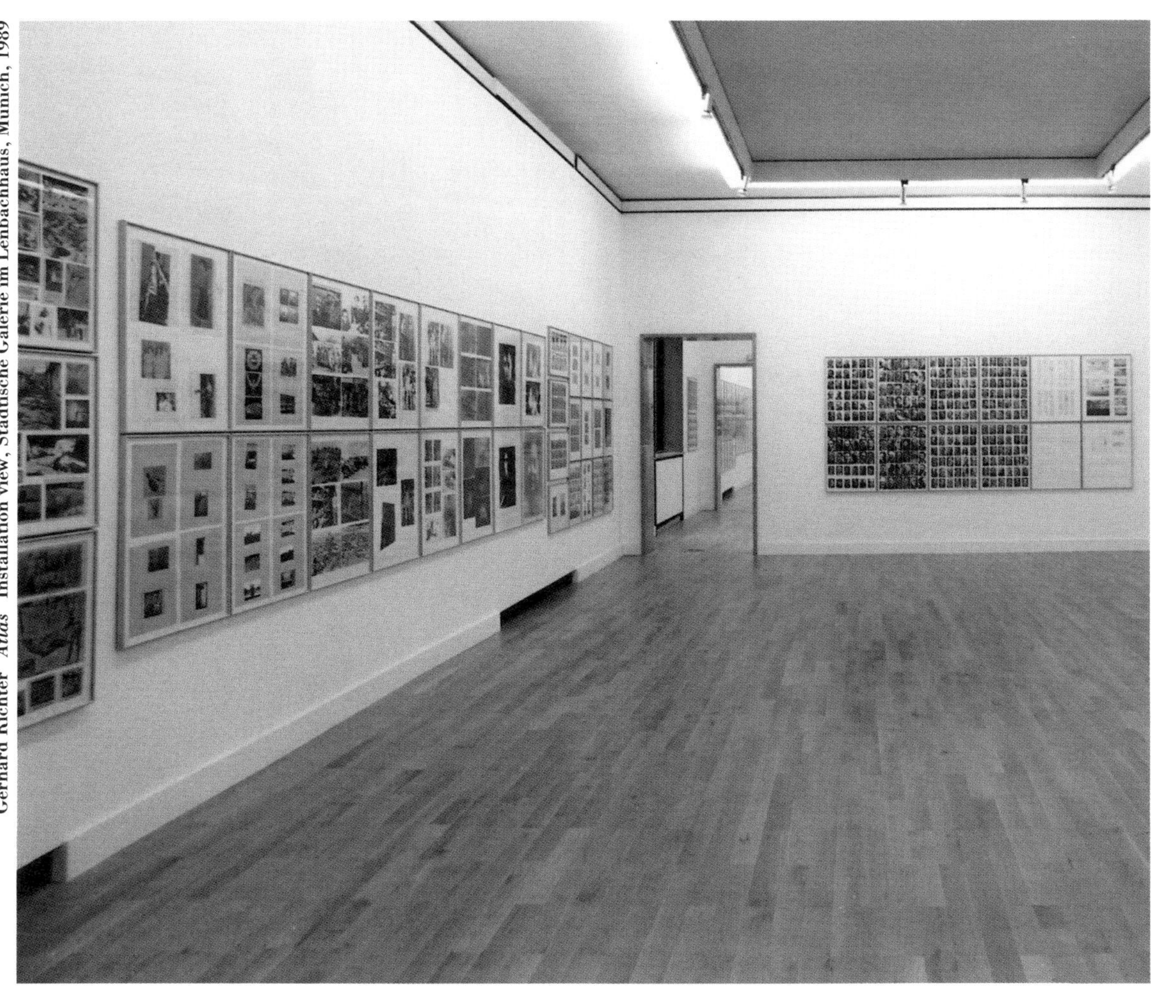

Gerhard Richter *Atlas* Installation view, Städtische Galerie im Lenbachhaus, Munich, 1989

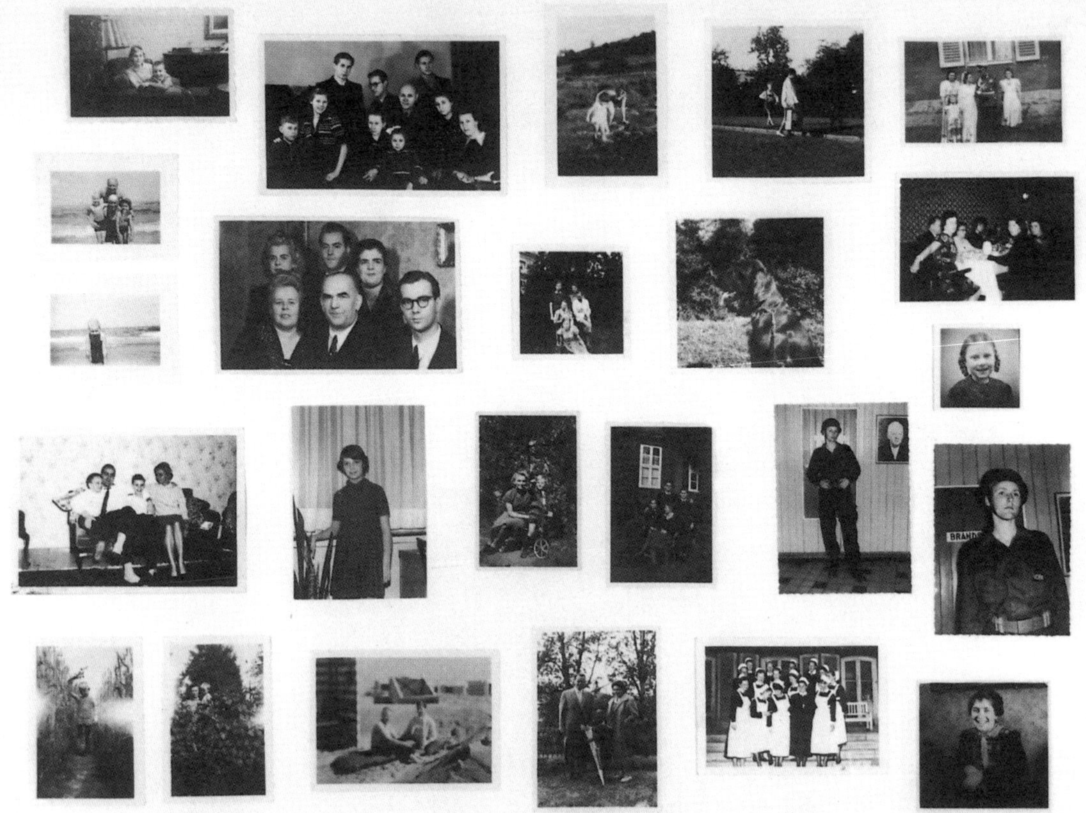

Gerhard Richter *Albumfotos (Album Photos)* 1962–1966 (from *Atlas*)

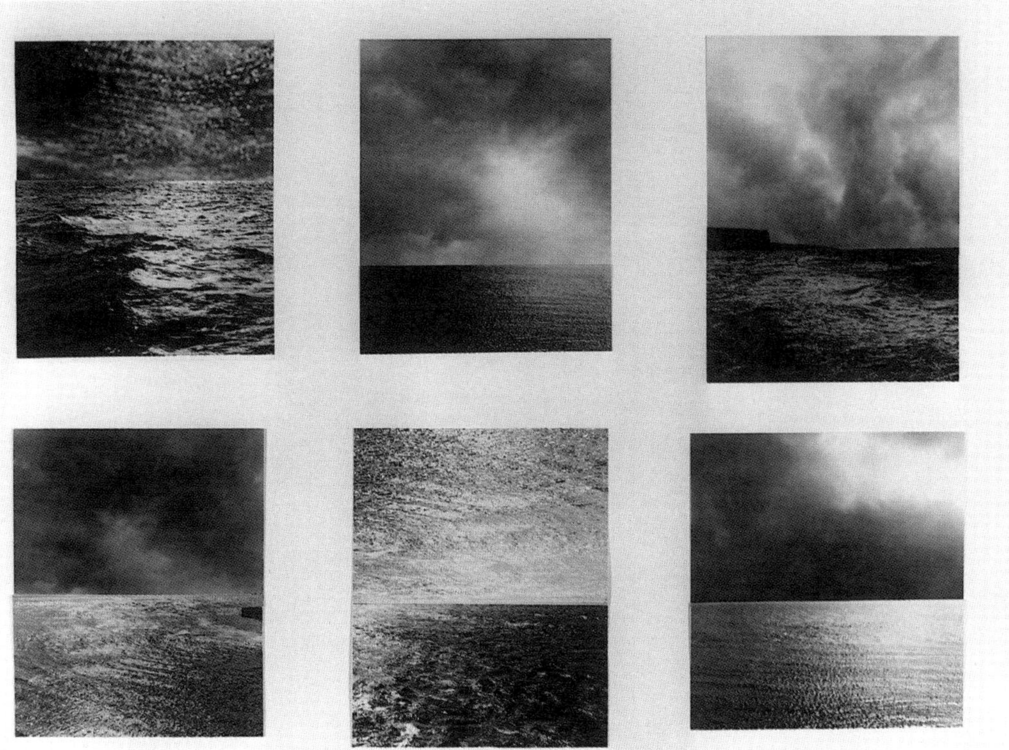

Gerhard Richter *Seestücke (Seascapes)* 1969 (from *Atlas*)

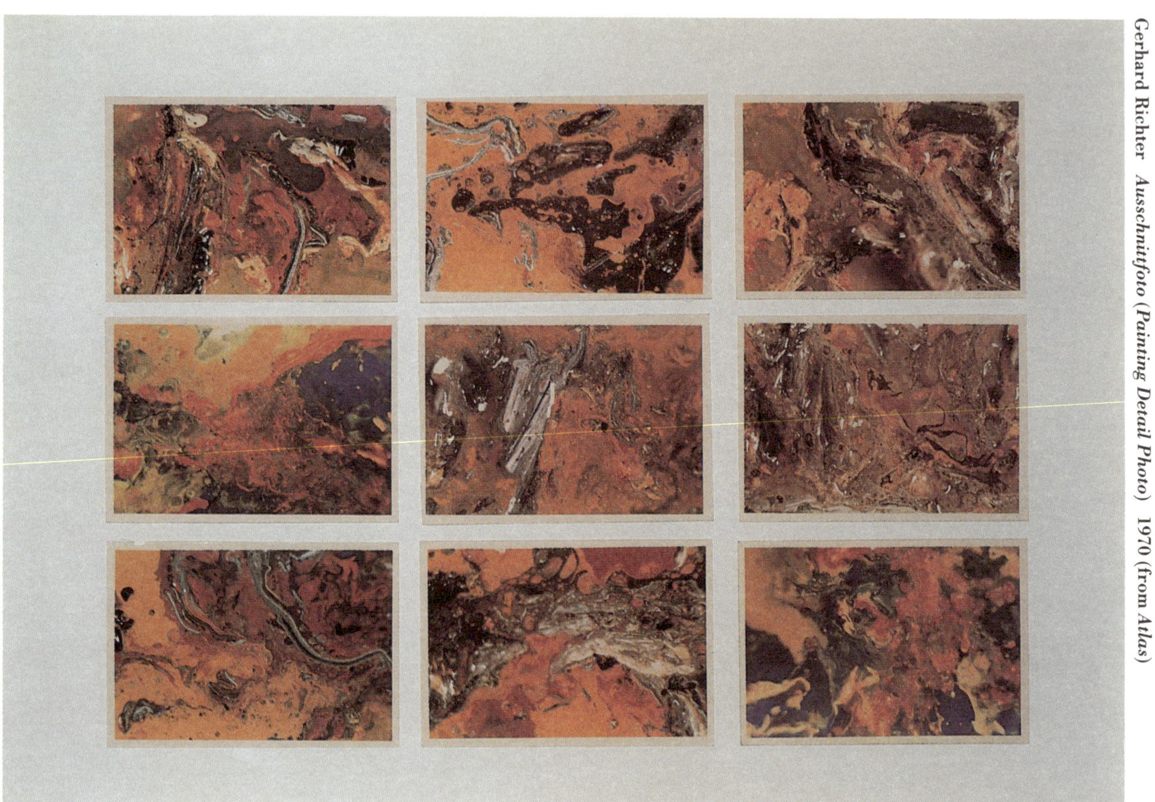

Gerhard Richter *Ausschnittfoto (Painting Detail Photo)* 1970 (from *Atlas*)

SIGMAR POLKE

Sigmar Polke is known primarily as a painter, but since the mid-1960s he also has produced an extraordinary body of photographic works. During the 1970s, in fact, photography constituted the primary focus of his activity. With the first large-scale exhibition of three decades of his photographic work in 1990 at the Kunsthalle in Baden-Baden, it became clear how critical the photographs are in his work and that he is equally a master of photography and painting. Seeing Polke's photographs reveals how slippery the distinction between the two media can be: he has subverted the mechanical intervention and distance of photography, just as he has challenged the handwrought quality of traditional painting. Polke sets up a continuum, exploring the outer extremes and overlapping edges of either medium, focusing on the way images are constructed and on the disparate readings and meanings that are possible.

The early photographs from the 1960s are seemingly casual but are in fact carefully constructed; they are humorous, ironic, iconoclastic, immediate, and modest. Polke is playing games, making puns, entertaining himself and his audience. Yet the works have an underlying seriousness of intent, both as a critique and an antidote to the materialist obsessions of German society in the 1960s. They are homages to the imagination and spirit.

In the 1970s Polke set out on a number of journeys, spending time in New York City, Brazil, Afghanistan, and Indonesia on a search, it seemed, for an understanding and a conceptual tool that would enable him break through the shield of European civilization. He faced two dilemmas. The first concerned the theories of Sigmund Freud, who in the early part of the century had articulated what he saw as the central problem of Western culture and art: The accomplishments of the West were rooted in the suppression of the unconscious, the control of internal expressions, and the sublimation of the sexual impulse to ordered, rational achievements. Second, Polke saw that he stood in a long line of European artists, challenged and chained by the attainments of earlier generations. Civilization itself and the products of its history were the weights from which Polke sought to rise. By the 1980s he had embarked on a reappraisal of the history of Western art and civilization.

In the series Goya, Die Alten (Goya, the Old Women) (1982–1984), Polke dissects and experiments with the process of making art and, within art, the process of making meaning. For the series, he took photographs and procured X rays of a great Goya painting known by two titles, *Time* and *The Old Women with a Looking Glass* (1812, Musée des beaux arts, Lille, France). The technique of the X ray is, of course, a method of diagnosis usually associated with a hunt for the cause of ill health; here, Polke uses the X ray to determine the cause of society's ill health. His choice of a canvas by the Spanish artist, too, is a highly conscious one. For Goya in his own period was a highly engaged and vital social critic and, in his late work, an explorer of the dark forces of the human psyche. The painting Polke chose as a point of departure is of a type called the *vanitas*, a meditation on the fleeting time of human life, the allure and frailty of human beauty, and the sexual undertones that physical attraction implies. Polke decomposes the painting, so that a sense of decay, of evaporation, becomes unavoidable. He imposes optical tricks such as floating dots and orbs onto the surfaces, and these work like lenses that both reveal and distort the reality underneath. The dots also allude to photomechanical reproduction techniques, which break images down into patterns of dots. Polke blows the dots up, making them more abstract and self-conscious. In a medium not usually associated with the handmade, he likewise exposes the artist's hand, his signature, his style. He reveals the layers out of which the image is constructed, the fluids out of which materials and images are composed in the photographic medium.

The thin line separating ecstasy (the unbridled freedom of imagination) and the abyss of terror (the awesome fright of emptiness) is apparent in these pictures. The pleasures and the pains of insight are shown to overlap, to occur simultaneously; any separation between the two is seen as momentary and illusory. Polke questions and celebrates the division between art and artifice, between profundity and superficiality, between the life of the mind and that of the body. No dichotomies and no easy distinctions can be maintained. He suggests that the truth of art, its power, lies in its ability to make visible what has been invisible, and he knows that the process is never complete.

Painting with oil glazes was developed by Flemish artists in the 1420s, catching light and infusing it into the colored paint surface. Photography was invented simultaneously by Daguerre and Fox Talbot, with two different processes, in 1839 in England and France. In Polke's work, neither painting nor photography is seen as superior; each simply bears different properties that have been developed with various conventions and histories. Polke is not content to let past assumptions about the two media dictate what is possible in the present. The relationship of the photograph to light and to the material and chemical properties of its making carries with it as many possibilities as does that of painting. Polke expands the sense of potential for both media.

Sigmar Polke *Röntgenbilder des Goya-Gemäldes* Die Alten (*X rays of Goya's Painting* The Old Women) n.d. fifteen X rays 69 1/4 x 50 3/4 in. (overall)

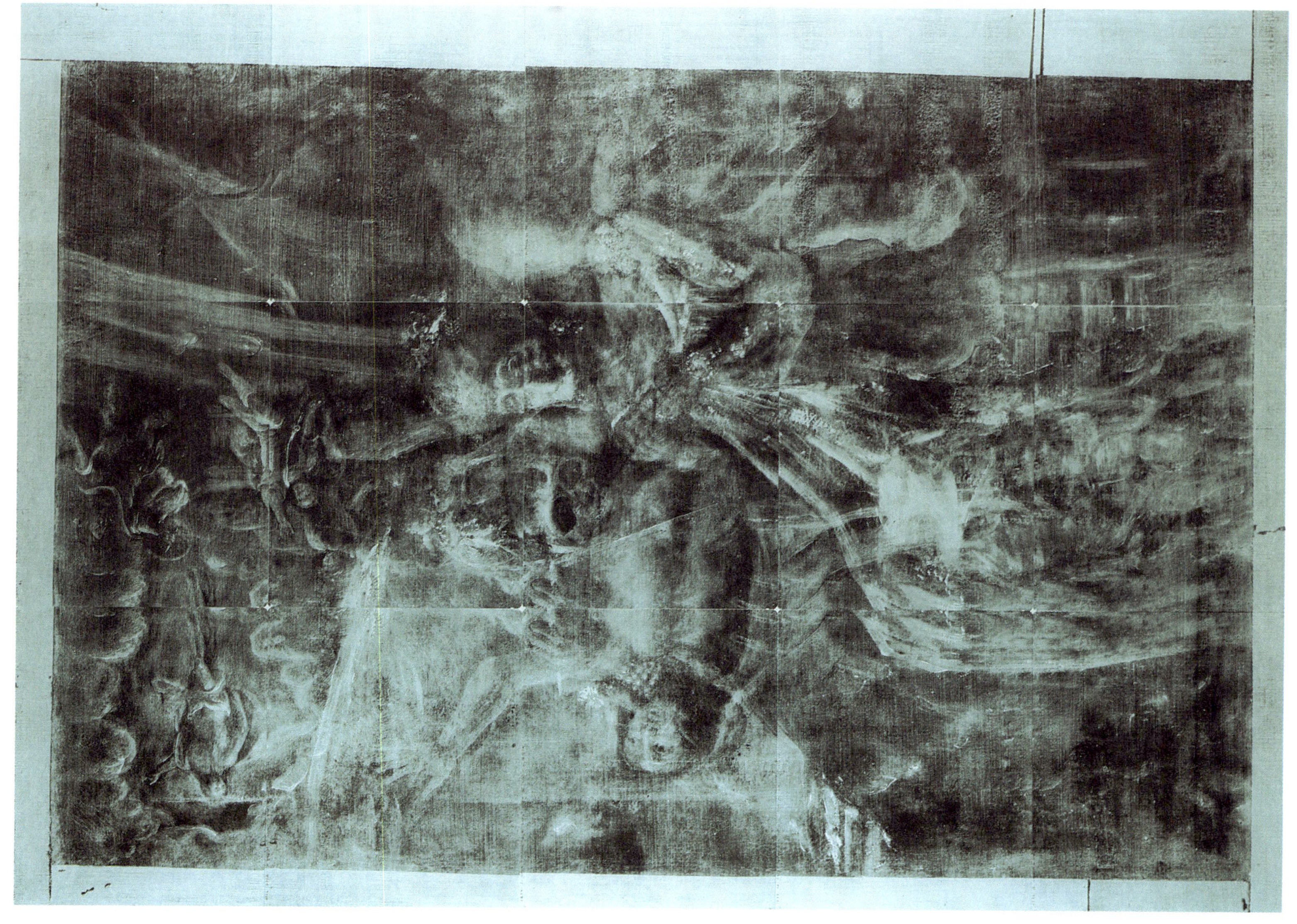

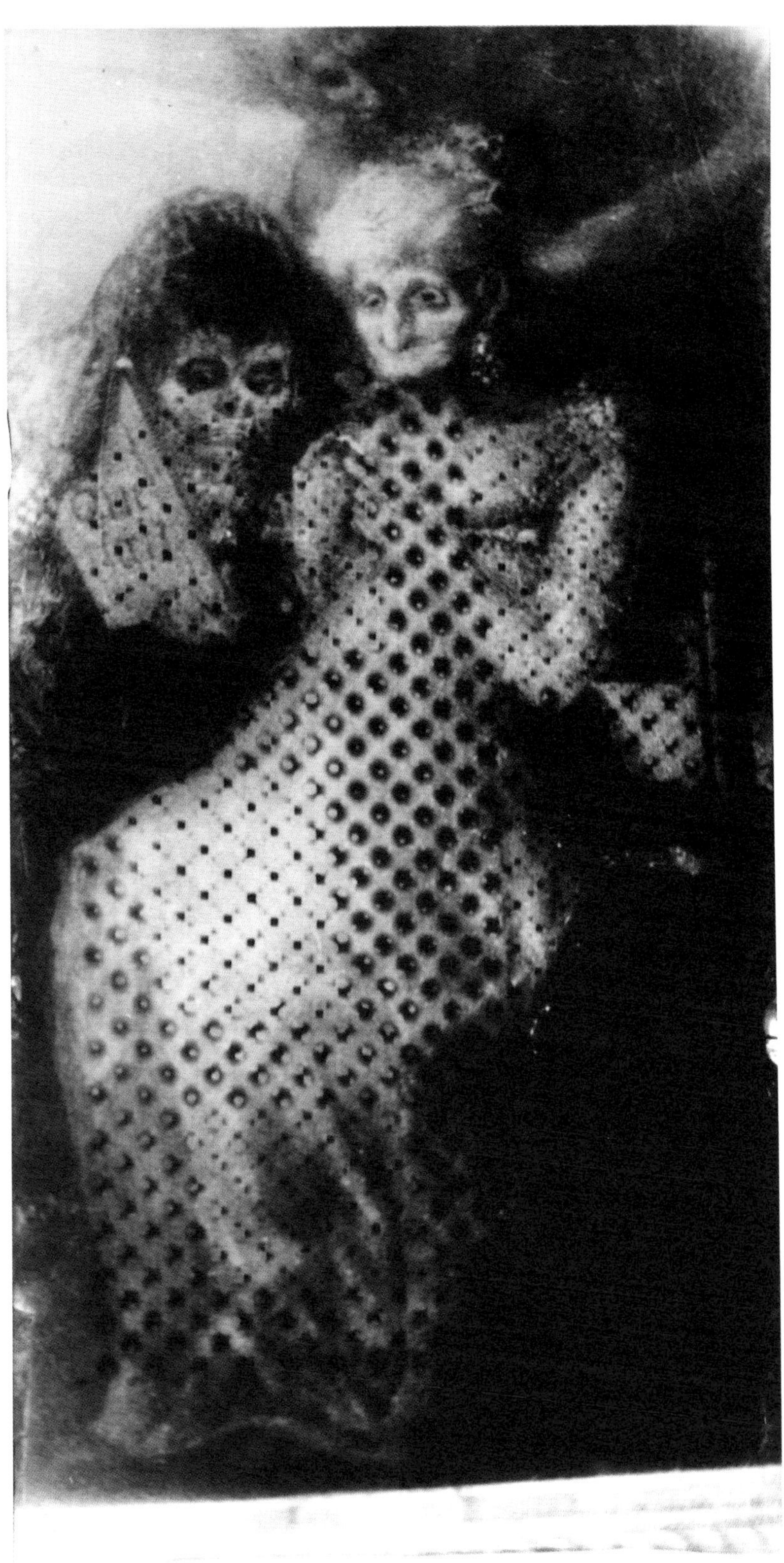

Sigmar Polke *Goya (Die Alten) (Goya [The Old Women])* 1984 photograph with photoengraving 100 3/8 x 50 in.

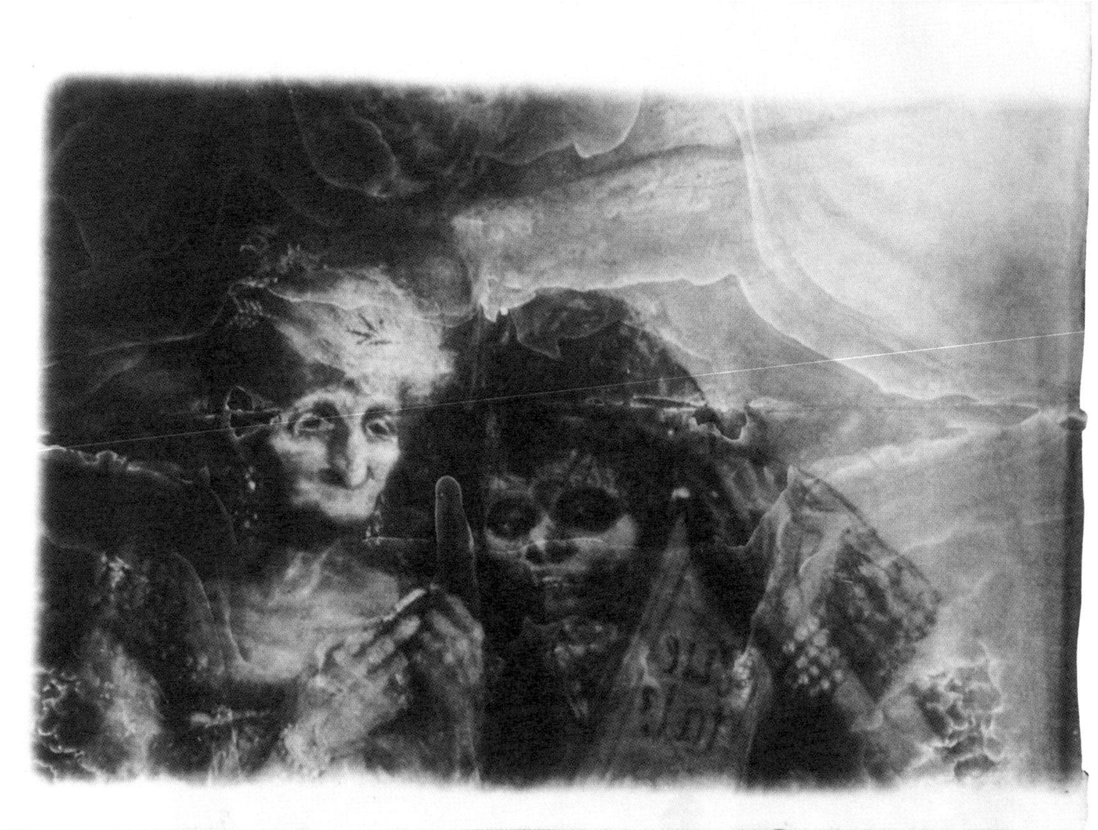

Sigmar Polke *Goya (Die Alten) (Goya [The Old Women])* 1984 photograph 50 x 70 5/8 in.

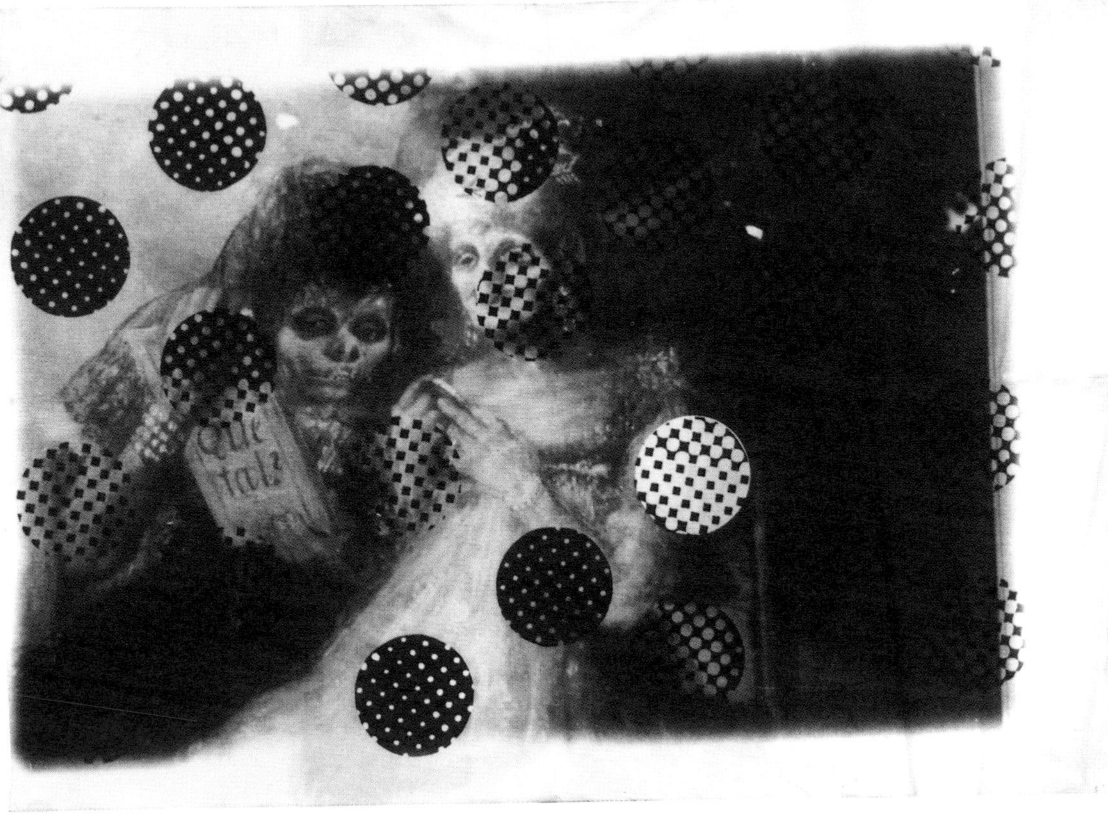

Sigmar Polke *Goya (Die Alten) (Goya [The Old Women])* 1984 photograph with photoengraving 50 x 72 5/8 in.

PETER ROEHR

Roehr's career spans the short period from 1962, the year of his earliest work, to 1968, the year of his death at age twenty-four. He worked in Frankfurt and, although he lacked extensive international connections, he independently advanced many of the strategies of Minimal and Conceptual art of the mid-to-late 1960s. While comparisons might be made between his work and that of Andy Warhol, he was not aware of Warhol until after he had begun his own production; moreover, he found the American artist's treatments overly romantic and traditional.

Strictly speaking, most of Roehr's works are not photographs, but they do use photographic images; most should be referred to as *Foto-Montagen* (photomontages). These are composed of grids of exactly identical photomechanical reproductions — generally advertising prints and proofs — that do not contain even the slightest trace of variation that can occur between photographic prints made from the same negative. Roehr would use these reproductions just as they were printed, without any editing or cropping, thereby pushing the idea of the photographic image to its most impersonal and mechanical end. He hoped to create work that would be as empty as possible of interpretive or subjective meanings. Parallel to the photomontages, Roehr made film montages from television commercials. He chose commercially produced images in part because he felt they were more public than pictures made or photographs taken by the individual artist and would thus have a less private or subjective character.

Roehr was interested neither in the individual subject or composition of an image nor in creating an overall pattern that would obliterate the single image. Rather, he wanted to make work in which the pattern of images would create a whole and in which the individuality of each small image could still be kept in focus. The capacity of the photographic image for absolute replicability opened up the possibility of a new kind of composition, of a new balance within the whole as a sum of its parts.

While using found reproductions, however, Roehr also was experimenting with the photographic medium itself. For a group of early works called *Lege-Montagen* (laid-down montages), he arranged a number of identical objects, such as coins, and took photographs of them, varying the light, thus allowing comparisons in the photographs between these objects. He also made four early *Foto-Montagen* using actual photographs rather than mechanical reproductions; in this case, he made two such works and then two more "identical" works.

Although Roehr's primary interests were conceptual and formal, his work is not without social implications and connections. His images are drawn from advertising brochures that celebrated the materialistically oriented society of 1960s Germany, the period when the so-called Economic Miracle was taking hold. Unlike many artists who were profoundly uncomfortable with this society, Roehr seemed to understand its potential for liberating the country from the constraints of prewar social values. In keeping with his perception of this potential, he sought to find an art that would not be tied to or weighed down by art-historical traditions.

Today, a quarter-century after Roehr's death, his works continue to be fresh and vivid. They are simple and direct, yet carry rich visual power. Their significance remains to be fully comprehended.

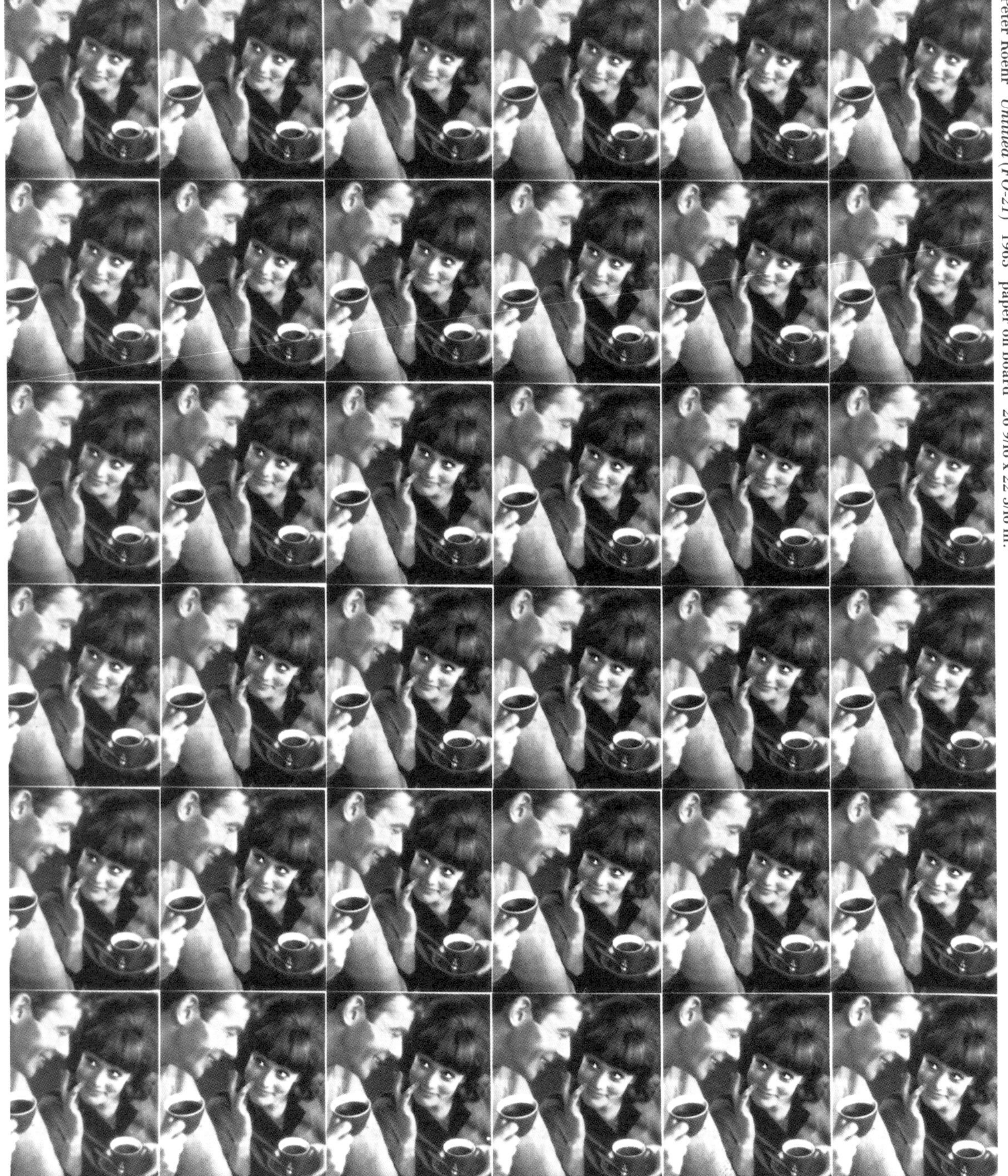

Peter Roehr *Untitled (FO-21)* 1965 paper on board 26 9/16 x 22 5/16 in.

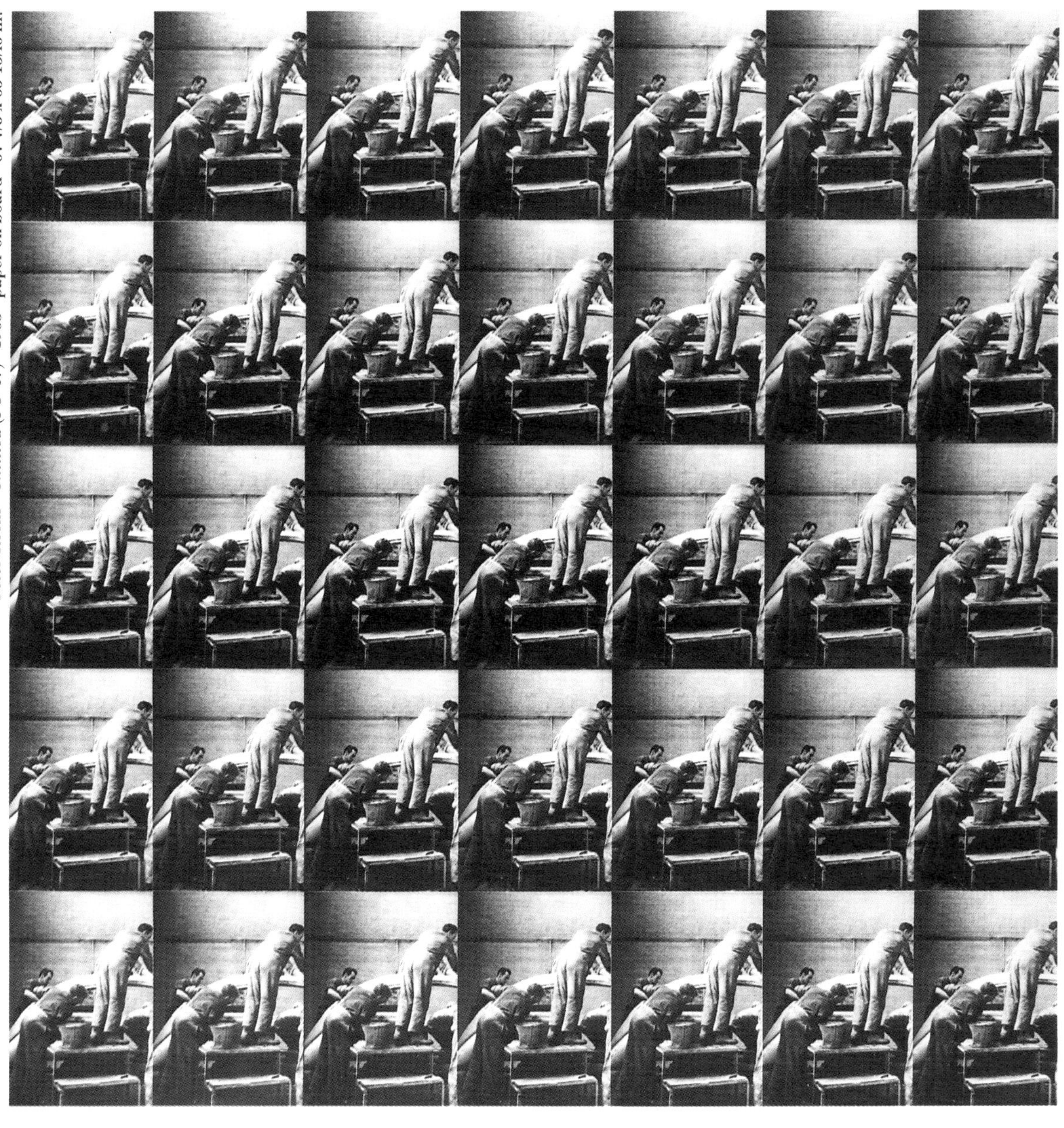

Peter Roehr *Untitled (FO-47)* 1965 paper on board 67 7/8 x 65 15/16 in.

Peter Roehr *Untitled (FO-83)* 1966 paper on board 16 15/16 x 17 9/16 in.

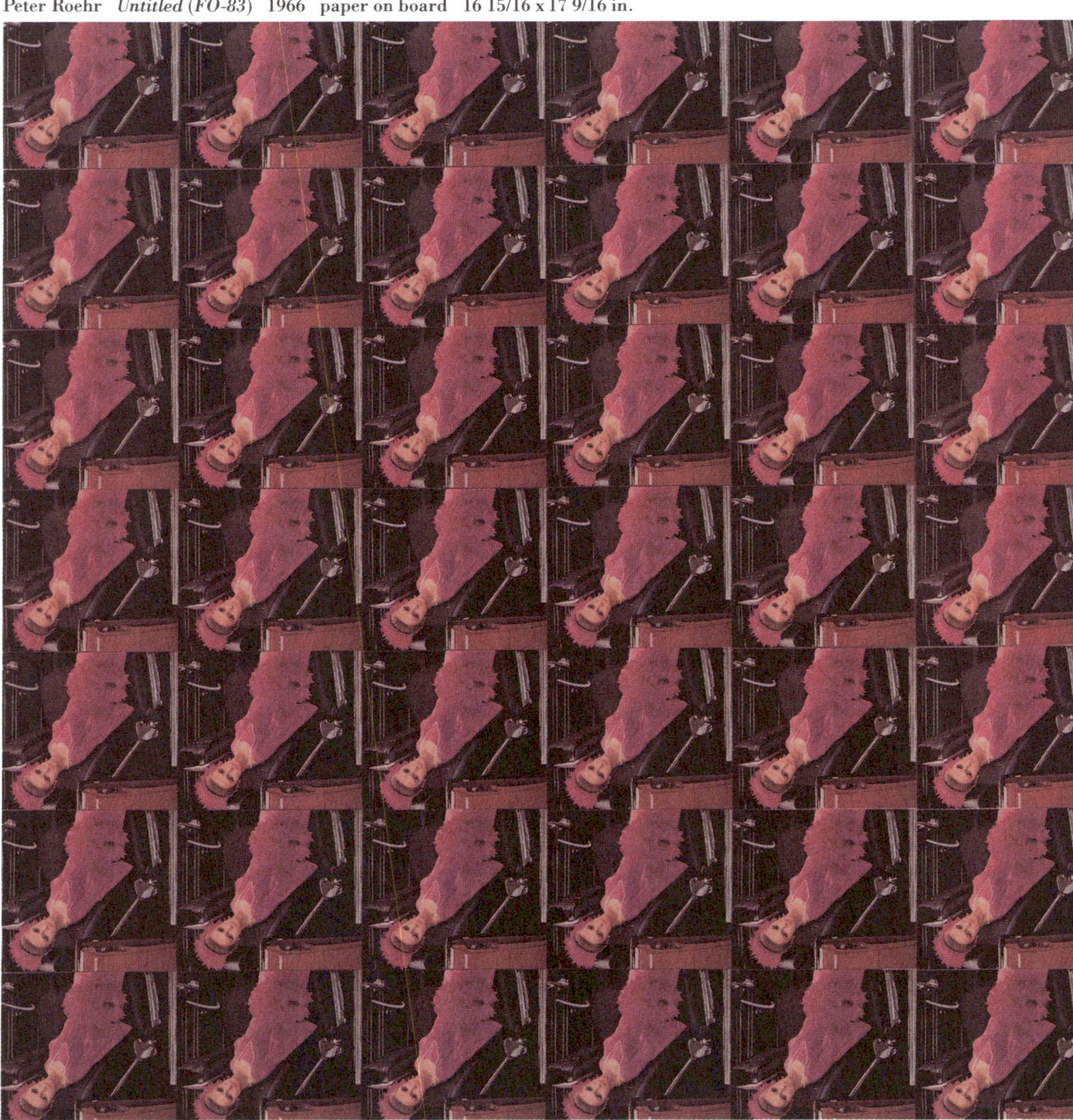

IMI KNOEBEL

Like Sigmar Polke and Gerhard Richter, Imi Knoebel began making art in the early 1960s in Düsseldorf while studying at the art academy there. He was a pupil of Beuys, and similarly, he has avoided defining his work by medium. Individual works occupy positions on a continuum running between architecture, sculpture, painting, and drawing. Drawing itself should be understood in an expansive way in his work to include not only works on paper — penciled line markings, collage, and photography — but also the physical arrangements of objects. Knoebel's work, however, has been primarily abstract, with space — and its links to color and light — being the central subject. He usually works in series, with related works often made over a period of years. All of his works share common concerns, conceptually and formally, and they explore the physical properties of a medium in relation to space and perception.

In the first half of the 1970s Knoebel was particularly involved with projections, creating works primarily through the medium of light. In 1970 he began this work with exterior projections but then moved into interior spaces, projecting large geometric forms with bright white light and giving them an almost physical presence. Later, in 1975, he used these projections as the basis for a series of paintings entitled Constellations — large, irregular white panels presented in groups that appeared almost to hover on the wall. His choice of the word *constellations* reveals an important way to view Knoebel's works: as embodiments of the apparitions of light, as a means of understanding the capacity of light both to reveal an object by catching its surface and to conceal an object by dissolving the surface. The title also suggests an open-ended system, in which connections may be understood by perception and agreement rather than by an absolute relationship.

In 1970 Knoebel also began using projections as a basis for making photographs, a series of works he would continue through 1975. To make his photographic works, he would blacken groups of glass slides, sometimes partially and sometimes completely. In some series, Knoebel would begin with projections of geometrical forms — translucent areas left in the black-painted slides — onto street-scapes or interiors and then take photographs of them. More frequently, he would completely blacken the slide glass and then scratch through the opaque surfaces, leaving fine lines or stippled breaks. He would then project each slide onto a wall and take a photograph of each of the projections. In some cases, he would move the projector slightly and take the photograph, catching the subtle, changing distortion of light. Knoebel explored many variations in this method of making photographs and produced thousands of individual negatives. Once a series of photographs was printed, he would present them together in a grid format. The grid is a form of presentation that emphasizes the momentarily fixed or static quality of our perceptions, captured from a condition of constant change and flux. Light itself, whether from the sun or the stars, is seen at a remove from its origin, both in time and in space. The photograph becomes a primary tool for catching and recognizing the nature of light and perception, and for understanding that both are always and simultaneously abstract and material. The photographs are one means by which Knoebel explores form as both negative and positive surface and space.

Knoebel's photographs were an important base for many series of works he made in other media in the 1970s and 1980s — not only the Constellations noted earlier — and they hold a crucial position in any consideration of his work. They also should be seen to have an important place in the history of twentieth-century German photography, as they extend the tradition of experimental abstract photography initiated by the avant-garde in Germany at the Bauhaus. The Bauhaus works, however, tended to be elaborately composed, singular images, whereas Knoebel's build on the practices of Conceptual Art of the late 1960s, which emphasized process, simplicity and directness of execution, and serial permutations. In a unique way, Knoebel's photographs fuse the elegance and mystery of modernist photography with the intellectual rigor of Conceptual Art.

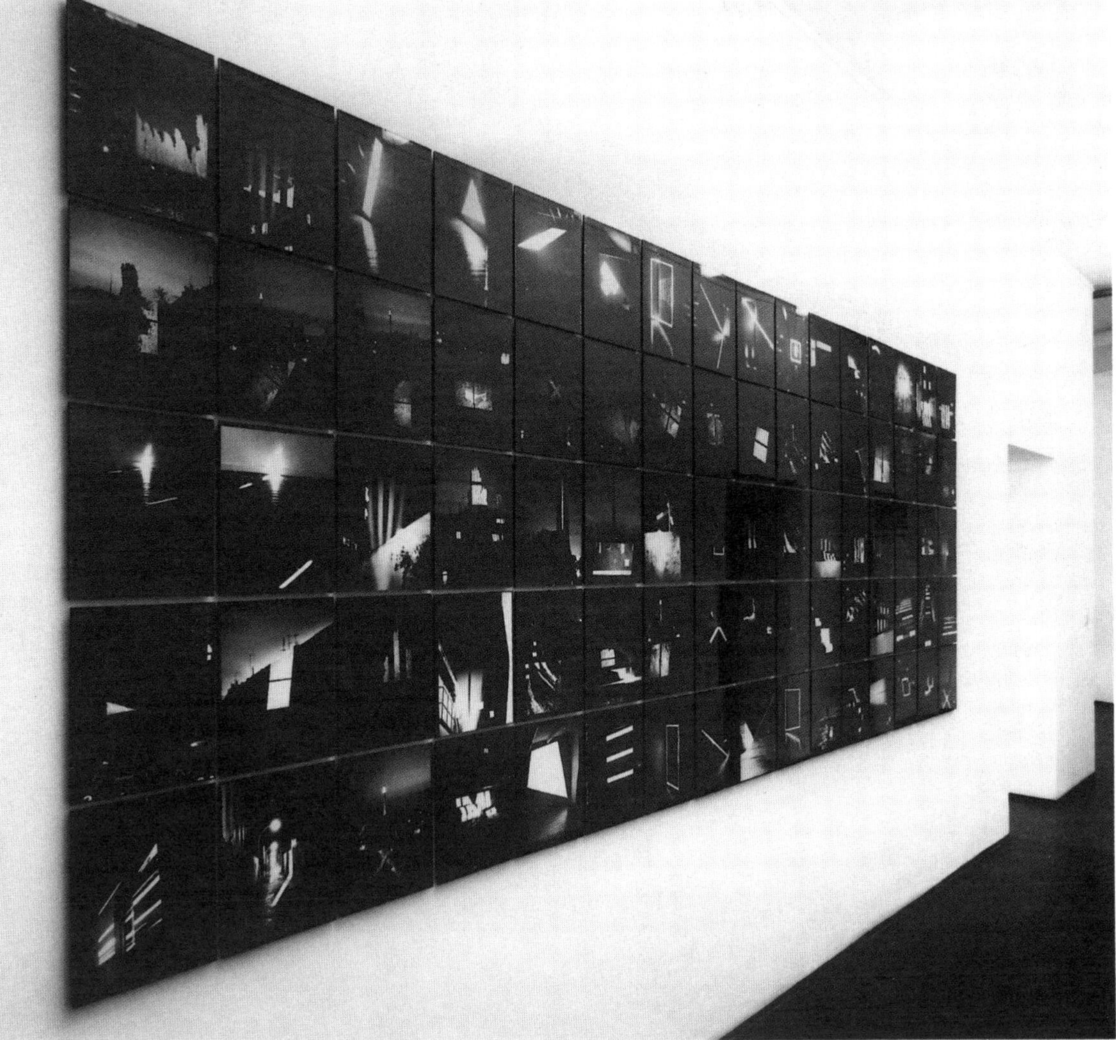

Imi Knoebel *Aussenprojektion (Exterior Projection)* 1971 Installation view, Galerie Heiner Friedrich, Cologne

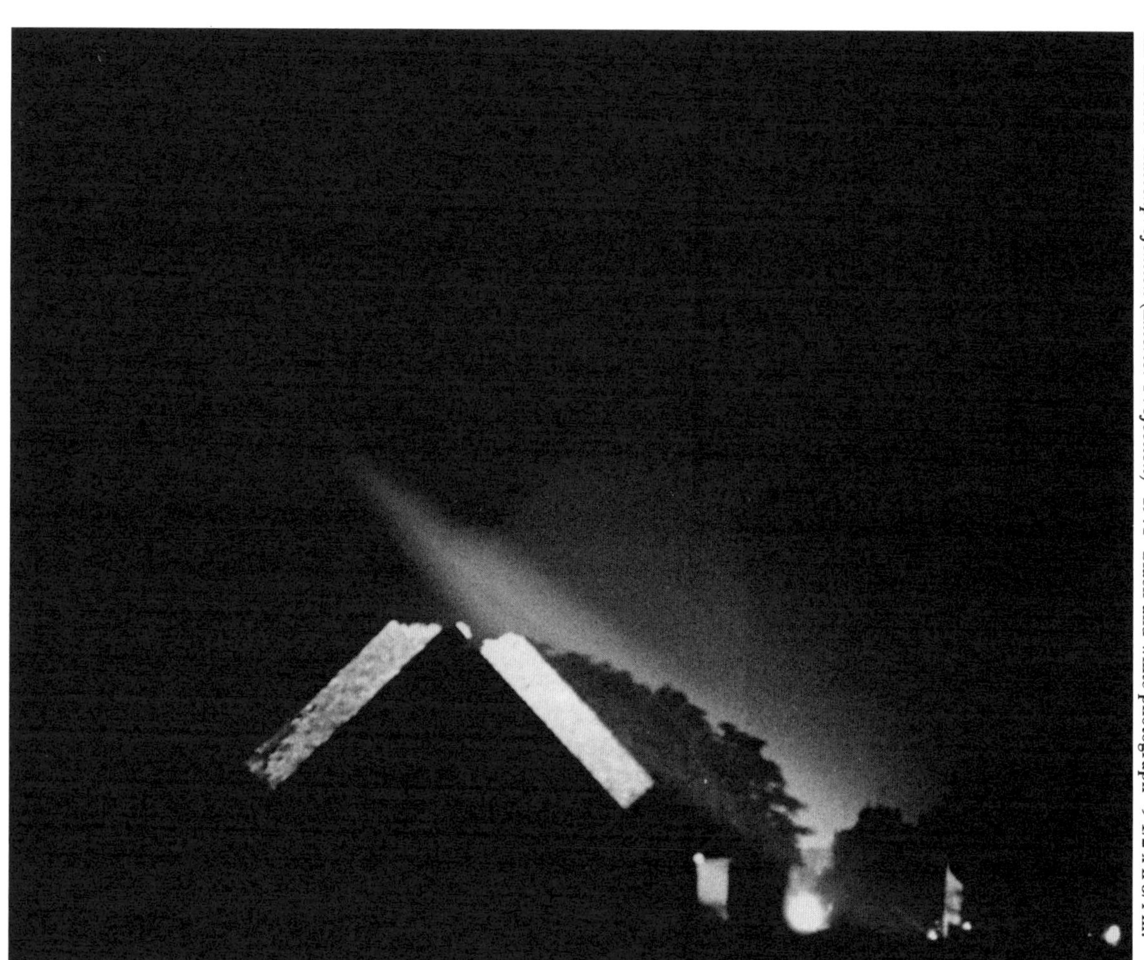

Imi Knoebel *Aussenprojektion (Exterior Projection)* 1971 black-and-white photograph 9 1/2 x 11 3/4 in.

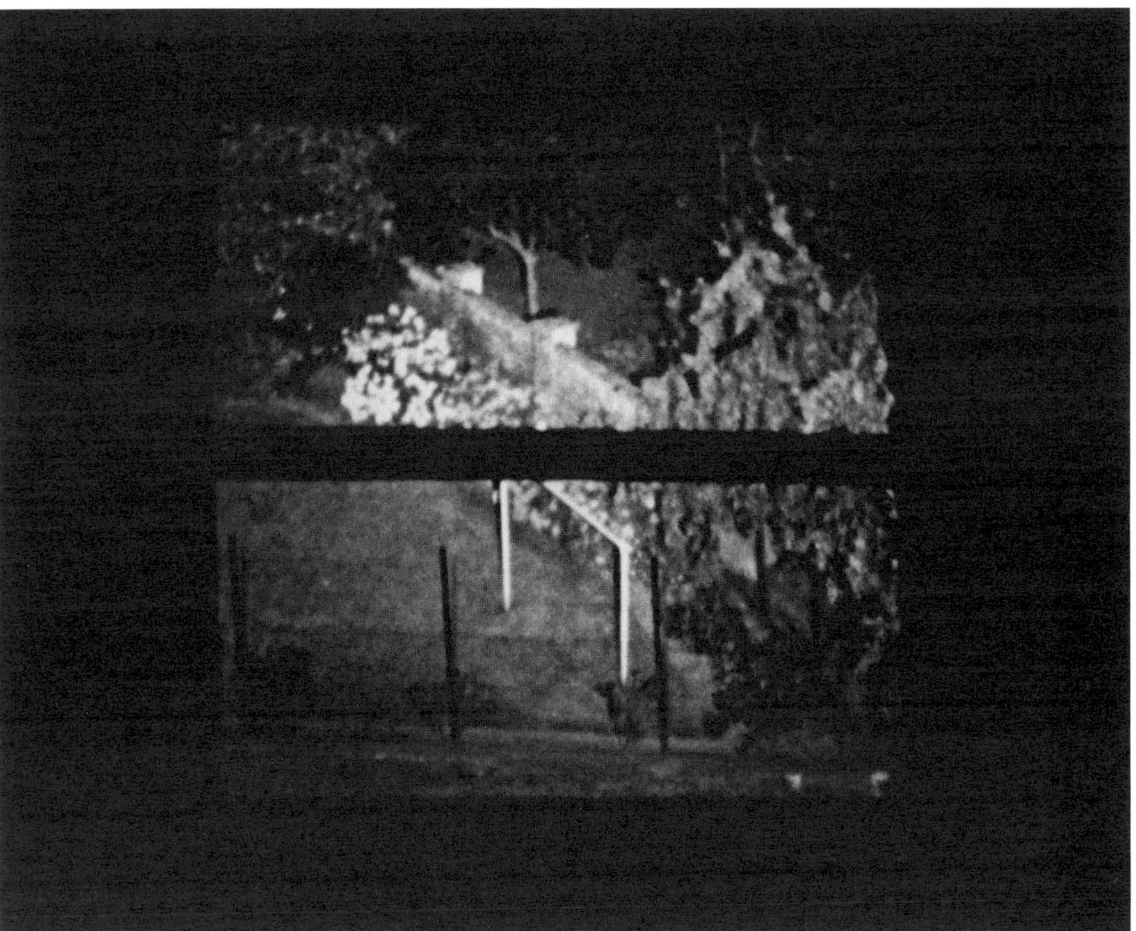

Imi Knoebel *Aussenprojektion (Exterior Projection)* 1971 black-and-white photograph 9 1/2 x 11 3/4 in.

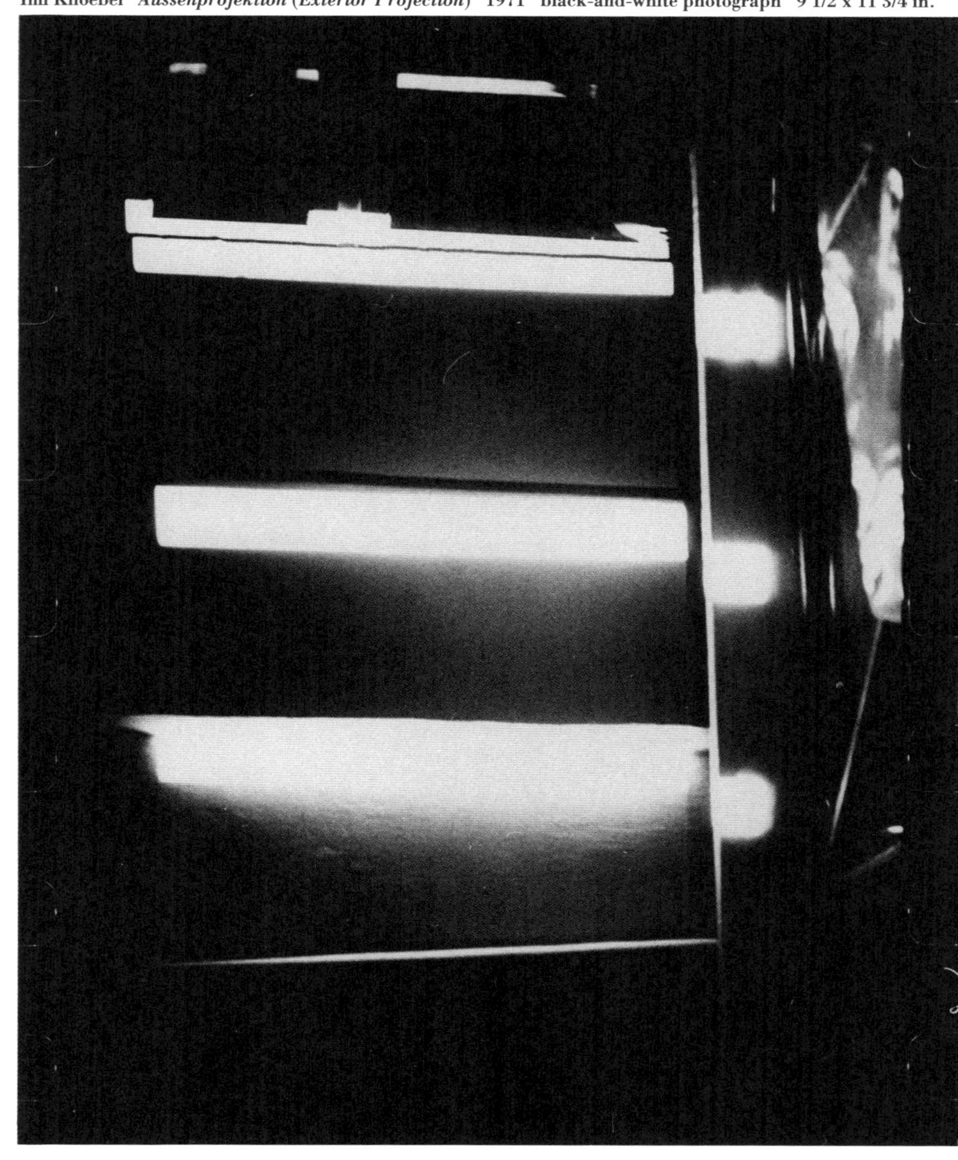

Imi Knoebel *Aussenprojektion (Exterior Projection)* 1971 black-and-white photograph 9 1/2 x 11 3/4 in.

HANNE DARBOVEN

Hanne Darboven was raised in Hamburg and came to New York City in 1965. There, she became close friends with the American artist Sol LeWitt. At that time, LeWitt was developing an art form out of abstract rules and systems, replacing the expressive gestures of Abstract Expressionism with rational, neutral markings and arrangements. With LeWitt as her champion, Darboven emerged in the late 1960s as one of the leading practitioners of what came to be called Conceptual Art; and, since her return to Hamburg in 1969, she has been one of its principal proponents in German art.

In contrast to her American counterparts such as LeWitt, who explored formal systems based on mathematics or language, Darboven's preoccupation was with time. Her early work captured a particularly European anxiety first expressed after World War II through Existentialist philosophy and literature, and it relays a sense of general uneasiness about the meaning of an individual's existence in the world. Although retaining the image of the handmade gesture, she made that gesture regular and systematic. Composed of series of sheets of paper, which each day would be covered with a cursive scrawl, her works marked the passage of time. They were structured as an abstract but personal record, in counterpoint to the framework of the Gregorian calendar by which time has been measured in Western civilization for centuries. Arranged in grids, Darboven's sheets of abstract writing created a fragile and vulnerable, yet tenacious, presence, an elegant assertion of personal identity and control.

Increasingly in the 1970s, Darboven's work expanded to include a larger sense of engagement with society and history. In 1978, with a piece entitled *Age of Bismarck*, she introduced photographic images into her work. This also was her first piece to deal explicitly with a historical subject. From then until now her work has combined her signature scrawl and photographic images in a shifting balance, a synthesis of private record and social memory. Unlike the ongoing line of her writing, which expands into open-ended time, the photograph captures a single moment, a particular place or time. Her use of photographic images has been varied; sometimes she repeats, only one image throughout a work, either as a photograph or as an offset reproduction. One of her richest and most variegated use of images occurs in *Vier Jahreszeiten (Four Seasons)* (1981), in which images are not repeated but are used with extraordinary variety. She includes her own photographs, vintage nineteenth-century photographs, numerous contemporary and historical postcards, and covers from magazines and journals. In *Existenz* (1989) she abandons any direct writing and instead presents photographs of every page of her datebook journals from 1966 to 1988 over a year's time; her dense handwritten entries chronicle the events and people of each passing day. The use of the photograph appears to represent an objectification of time and the entry into history.

The work presented in this exhibition, *Kurt Schwitters* (1987), records the passage of days in that year, which was the centenary of Schwitters' birth. Since her return from New York City, Darboven has lived and worked in her family's house. The private part of her work has become this house, to which she has added rooms over the years, filling them with objects and in the process creating an environment akin in spirit to that of Schwitters' studio environments, which he called the *Merzbau*. Not so well-known as his collages, which, like Darboven's sheets, were publicly exhibited works, the *Merzbau* rooms were elaborate and fanciful, three-dimensional constructions that filled his living quarters. Tragically, they were destroyed during World War II after Schwitters had been forced to flee the Nazis. He died in England in 1948.

Darboven's homage to Schwitters is arranged by weeks, beginning on December 29, 1986, and ending on December 31, 1987. There is one numbered page for every day of the year, and each page is preceded by an additional index page for every week. Each index page includes two collaged photographs. One image, which remains the same throughout the work, shows Darboven's residence and studio from the exterior, the public view. The other image, which changes every week, shows different views of the interior, the private life. On each of the date pages is glued a printed postcard with a Kurt Schwitters commemorative postage stamp, and Darboven's home address is given as that of the sender. Below her address a brief score of musical notes is written. These are from a system of musical notations that she has developed out of her system of numbering dates and from which, since 1979, she has created scores for organ, string quartet, and chamber orchestra. In this way, too, Darboven finds common ground with Schwitters, who was well known for his sound poems. The work is both an homage and an identification with him as a fellow artist. It embeds the passing of each week of daily life in a larger historical frame, in which the individual's life is no longer under his or her direct control. The individual can create or find an index to the abstract systems of time and history but cannot finally escape from them.

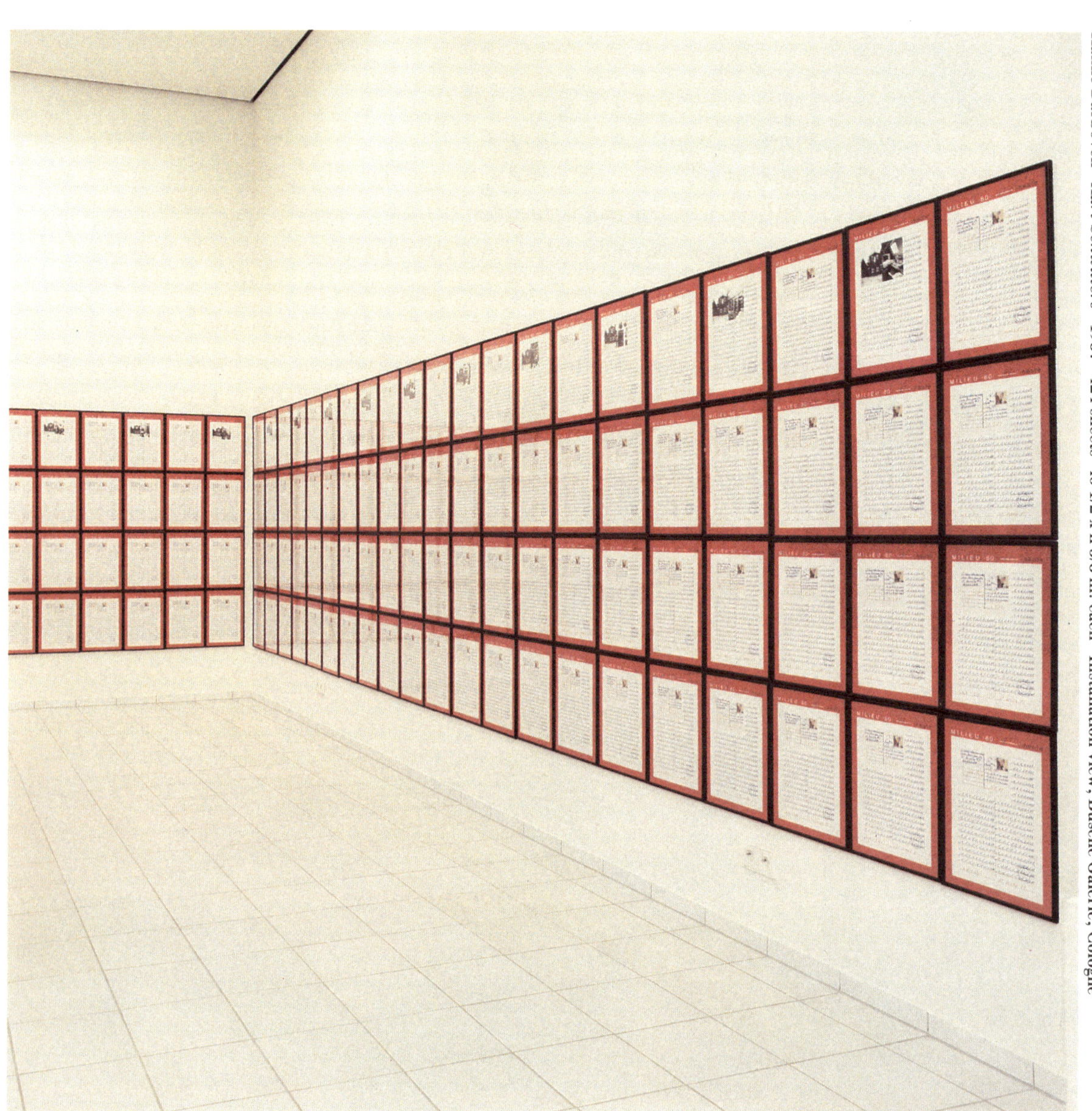

Hanne Darboven *Kurt Schwitters* 1987 424 sheets 16 1/2 x 11 5/8 in. each Installation view, Busche Galerie, Cologne

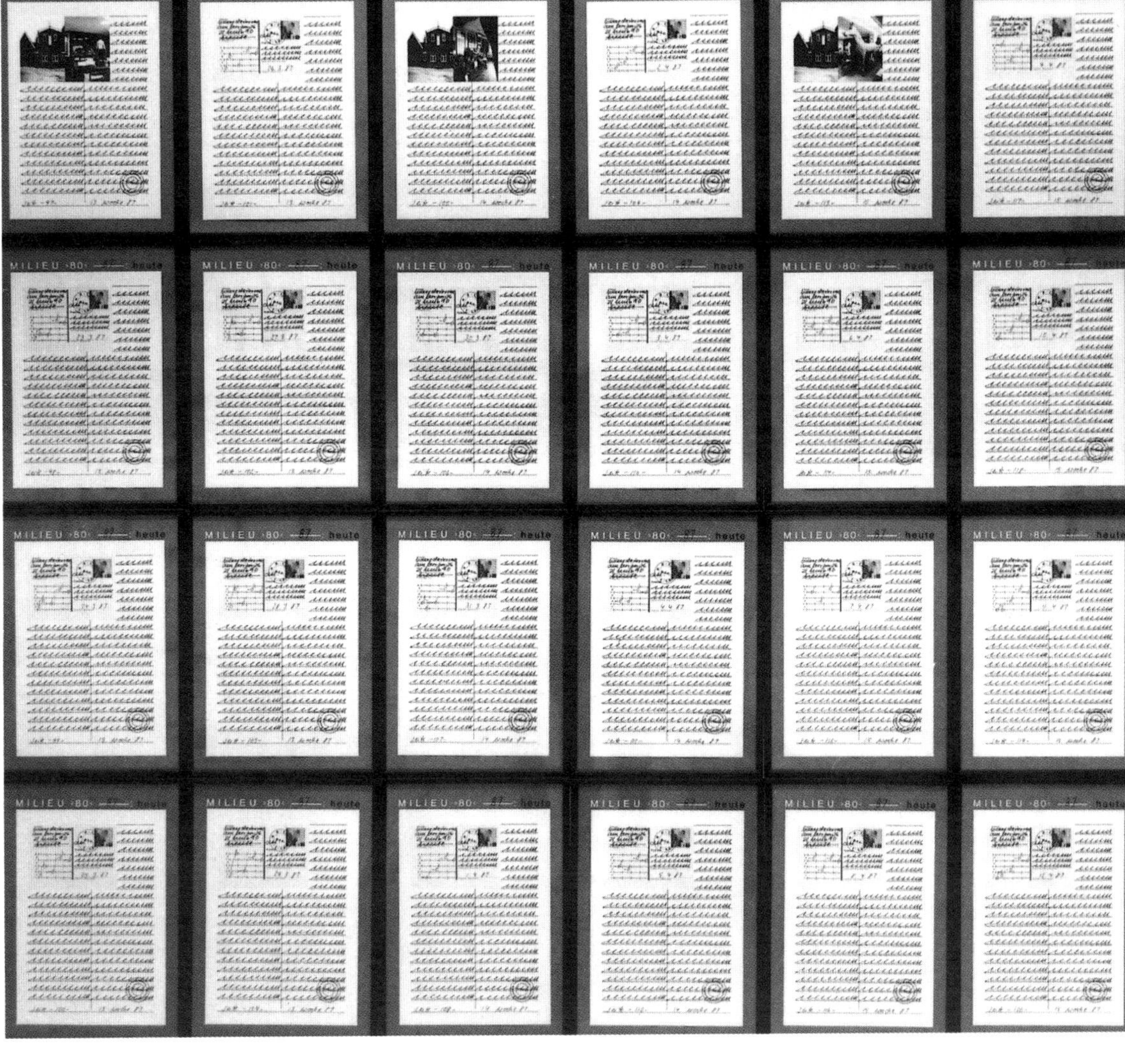

Hanne Darboven *Kurt Schwitters* 1987 (detail)

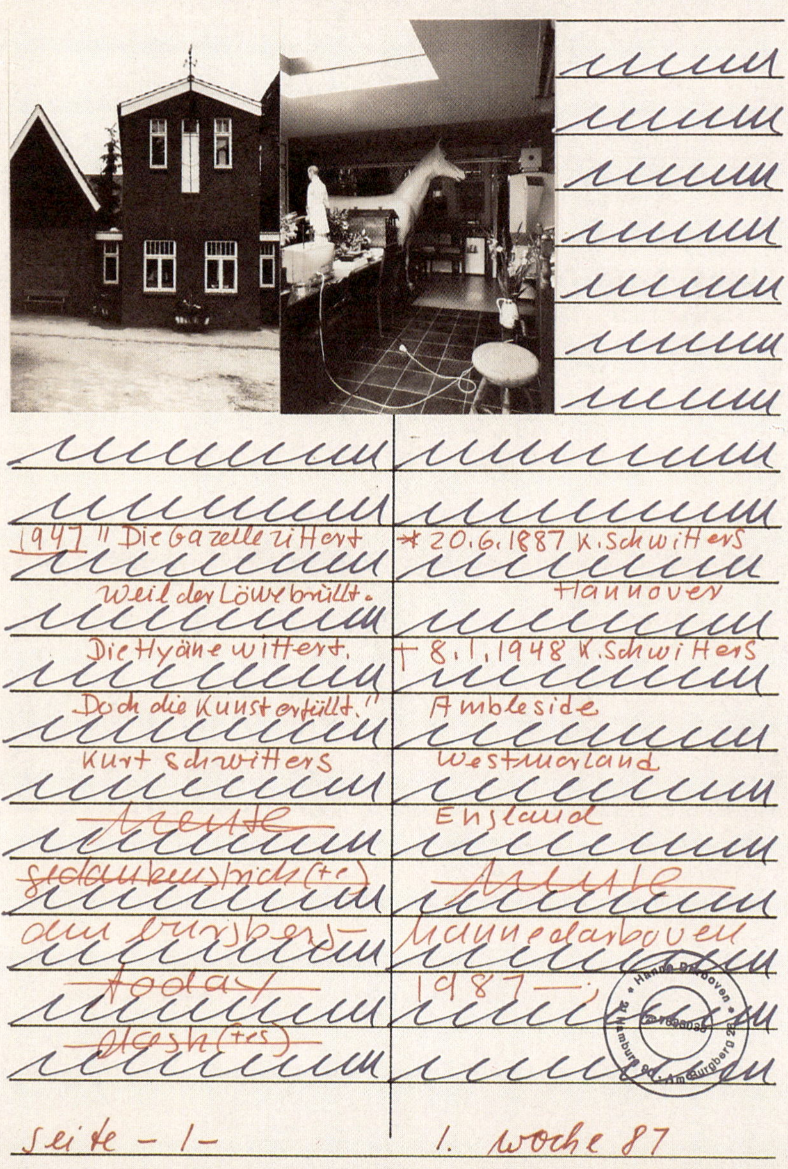

Hanne Darboven *Kurt Schwitters* 1987 (detail)

HANS-PETER FELDMANN

Hans-Peter Feldmann is little-known in the United States. He began working in 1968, producing the first of the small handmade books that would become a central part of his work. These books, simply entitled *Bild* or *Bilder* (*Picture* or *Pictures*), would include one or more reproductions from a certain category — airplanes, shoes, chairs, soccer players, landscapes, film stars — taken from various printed sources and made into a consistent format, their subjects centered and isolated and presented without captions. Despite their modesty, these books, made in unnumbered, open-ended editions, were produced with careful attention to subtle details of style and materials: they were hand-size in scale; their covers were made of heavyweight paper in various shades of gray with hand-stamped lettering; slightly grainy black-and-white reproductions were centered on the page. By the time he made his last such book in 1976, Feldmann had completed more than three dozen. They set the stage for a diverse body of related works, including printed books, postcard series, offset posters, hand-colored offset prints, and magazine and catalogue projects.

In part, the absence of recognition for his output has been due to the modesty of the work itself, its simplicity, its apparent ephemerality, and its lack of commercial value. In many ways his art is one of ideas rather than of production values. This may explain, too, why at the end of the 1970s he virtually ceased to make art or participate in exhibitions. At the end of that decade, large-scale painting and sculpture and market-driven evaluations began dominating contemporary art, and Feldmann withdrew. Not until very recently has he again begun to produce new work; one recent series, derived from images of the Eiffel Tower, is included in this exhibition.

Feldmann might be characterized as an artist's artist, making work for a small number of fellow connoisseurs. Yet he has not purposely positioned himself to have his work appreciated only by a few properly trained or educated specialists. On the contrary, he emphatically favors the democratic dispersal of images that has been a facet of late twentieth-century life. Like the American artists Edward Ruscha and Andy Warhol or artists in this exhibition such as Gerhard Richter and Peter Roehr,

Feldmann recognizes the problematic nature of pictures and art in a culture inundated by images. Photographic images disseminated through the media often appear to be random or spontaneous. An offhandedness often can be found in them. They do not have the scale, singularity, or preciousness — the greatness — associated with art. Yet, these pictures are intrinsically interesting: people have an almost insatiable appetite for them, poring through magazines, endlessly taking and saving family snapshots, collecting postcards and the like, and occasionally clipping an image to hang on a wall or post on a bulletin board.

Feldmann's response to all of this has been to celebrate the diversity and wealth of interesting pictures available through books, newspapers, magazines, postcards, calendars, announcements, and advertising. His speciality has been to heighten an appreciation of these images, to bring some order of understanding to them by removing them from the ordinary, day-to-day context in which they are first presented. He recognizes that often there are strong formal conventions and styles associated with media images. He overlays his own formal system on them, to give them a consistency and to allow comparisons. Feldmann subjects these images to scrutiny, revealing both the delight and pathos often contained in them. It is odd to recognize how often we are blind to the images that surround us, how blinkered our vision becomes as we shut out much of the visual barrage to which we are constantly subjected. Yet, Feldmann understands how wedded we have become to these images — the visual mirror to the world in which we live.

In making his modest but precious books, in issuing his sets of postcards, or in hand-coloring mechanically produced images, Feldmann in an understated way manages to recapture the potential power of images. He creates, in fact, fetish objects, giving back to the pictures a secret, almost magical aura. It is the tension he creates between the banal origins and functions of mass-produced photographic images and their potential for fascination that gives his work its power and appeal.

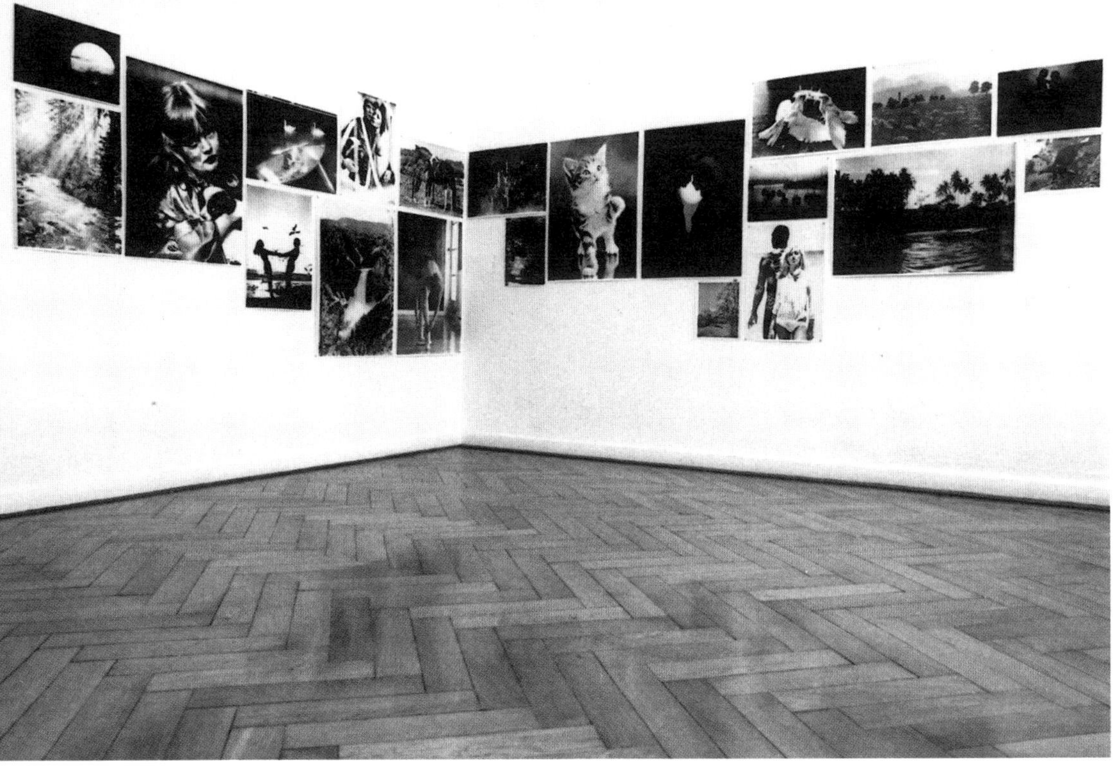

Hans-Peter Feldmann *Sonntagsbilder* (*Sunday Pictures*) 1976–1977 twenty-one black-and-white offset lithographs and screenprints on paper Installation view, Galerie Paul Maenz, Cologne

Hans-Peter Feldmann Bilder von Feldmann (Pictures by Feldmann) booklets by Feldmann presented in a cardboard case

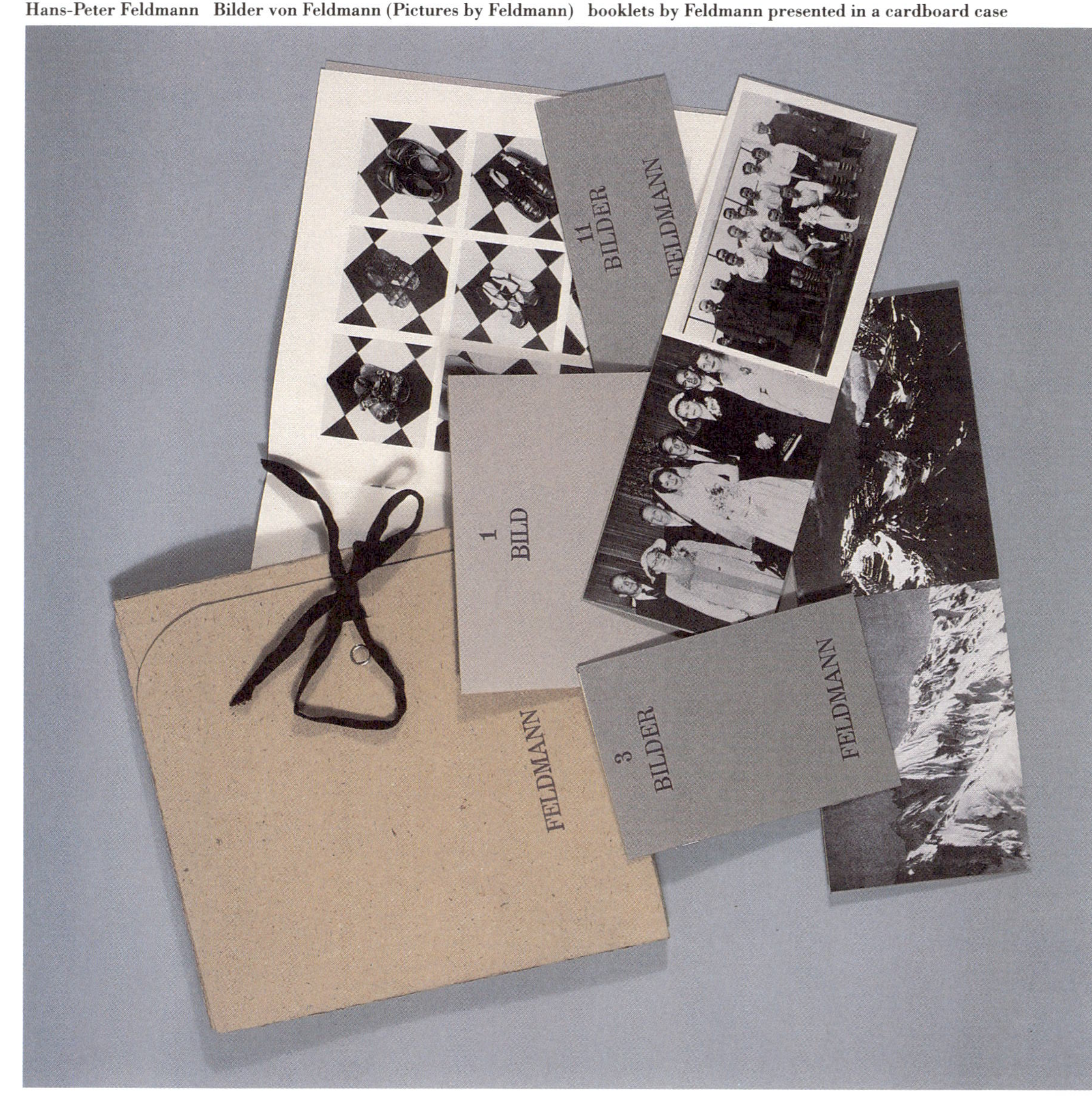

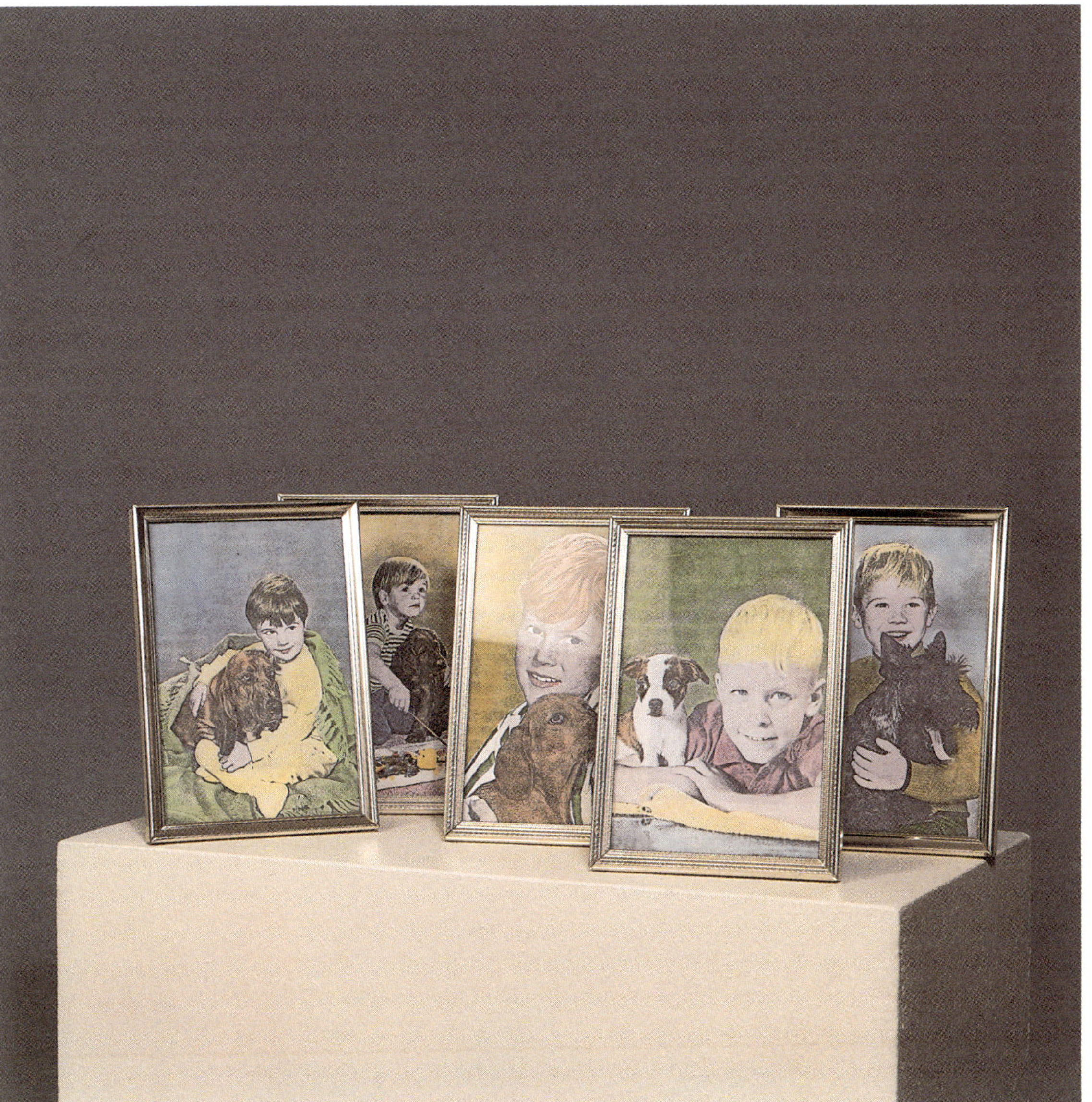

Hans-Peter Feldmann *Kinderfotos (Photos of Children)* 1977 five hand-colored photocopies in silver metal frames 5 3/4 x 4 in. each

ANSELM KIEFER

In the past two decades, Anselm Kiefer has established a reputation as a master of large-scale painting and unique handmade books. Some of his works may readily be categorized as paintings, sculptures, drawings, prints, collages, or books; many, however, fuse or resist these categories. Kiefer is well known for the variety of materials he uses — straw, sand, lead, and glass (among others), as well as paint and photographic prints. His nontraditional use of media and their rich formal combinations often make the usual labels inadequate. In Kiefer's work, the photograph is a consistent and central element, but it can probably best be understood as one more type of material, one with highly specific and peculiar properties.

Thus, a photograph often underlies even the largest of the so-called paintings, serving as a kind of underdrawing and ground onto which a wide array of other materials has been applied to create an overall pictorial and physical perception. Photographic vision — a one-point perspective — was devised in the Italian Renaissance of the fifteenth century, but it was only in the nineteenth century that technologies were developed to hold the image permanently on a surface, either paper or metal. Kiefer exploits the dramatic illusion of recession into deep space that is made possible with photographic vision, uniting that perspective with the materials and surface structure of abstract painting. In some cases, fragments of photographs are joined to the surfaces of these large works, further confounding the illusory properties of the image.

Photographs are most essential to the books Kiefer makes. In his earliest books, made in 1969, he often used himself as a staged subject of photographs that would be mounted to single sheets in handmade books. Through the 1970s the photographs and the books increased in complexity to include photographs of staged scenes in his studio interposed with scenes in the landscape. The photographs were of the same size as the book page, sometimes partially or fully covered over with a variety of paints and other materials. In a recent catalogue devoted to Kiefer's books, Götz Adriani has written: "Photographs, treated and manipulated in many different ways, are Kiefer's base. In his early books, he glued commonplace photographic motifs, series of photographs, or sections from catalogues that were so fragmented as to be unrecognizable, as well as bits of newspaper, in specific thematic and time sequences. Every transitory photograph, representative of reality at that given moment, visibly became the basis for that reality, and the various layers of materials applied to it derived meaning from their powerful energy. The traces of photographic juxtapositions on heavy paper are blurred by layers of oil, glue, acrylic, ink, coal, clay wash, ash, or sand, so that perception is filtered through substances that are, to a considerable degree, artistically fresh. Kiefer considers the photographs a provocative reality, layered with his reflections and feelings. Kiefer calls this work in transparent layers 'inverted archaeology.'"[1]

In the two-dimensional pieces often referred to as "lead works," thin lead sheets are often collaged with photographs. The color, texture, and reflectiveness of both photographs and lead create spatial and pictorial ambiguities, reinforcing the tension in these works between otherworldly mysticism and tenacious materiality. The photograph is light and illusory, while the lead has a heavy, obdurate physicality. The photograph is used as a fractured and tenuous window out of the frame, and the lead is often exploited for its dull but shimmering reflectiveness. The two materials would seem to be irreconcilable, but in Kiefer's work they are fused, eerily, to complement one another.

Kiefer consistently explores questions of memory, history, and myth, often making allusions to German history, particularly to the Nazi period. Birth and death, destruction and regeneration are frequent themes, reflecting Aryan mythology. Kiefer has delved in recent years into world culture to develop these inquiries, including the Hebrew story of Lilith and the Egyptian story of Isis and Osiris, into his work. His approach is less one of making isolated, iconic works than it is the creation of thematic series, so that many works and types of works may deal with a single theme. Sometimes the same photographic image is used with various media, or is used more than once over a period of years. Within individual pieces, a strong sense of story and narrative is felt. The books, particularly, with their capacity to hold incidents or frames within a single work, are a logical preoccupation for Kiefer and are among his most important works.

Kiefer is now at work on his first film, *Noch ist Polen nicht verloren* (*Poland Is Not Yet Lost*), tracing a theme with which he first worked in the late 1970s in painting. His attraction to film is an outgrowth of his work with books and photographs. As the curator John Neff has written: "With changing vantage points, cuts, closeups, and other techniques calculated to bring the viewer into the flow of events, Kiefer has given these books a strong cinematic feel, a quality only enhanced by the dramatic lighting, and model objects and landscapes he uses on the studio set where many of his photographs are taken."[2] Kiefer's new work in film extends the physical and narrative qualities consistent in all of his work — with the photographic medium at its heart.

1 Götz Adriani, ed., *The Books of Anselm Kiefer, 1969 – 1990*, trans. Bruni Mayor (New York: George Braziller, 1991), p. 12.

2 John Hallmark Neff, "Reading Kiefer," *Anselm Kiefer: Bruch und Einung*, exh. cat. (New York: Marian Goodman Gallery, 1987), p. 9.

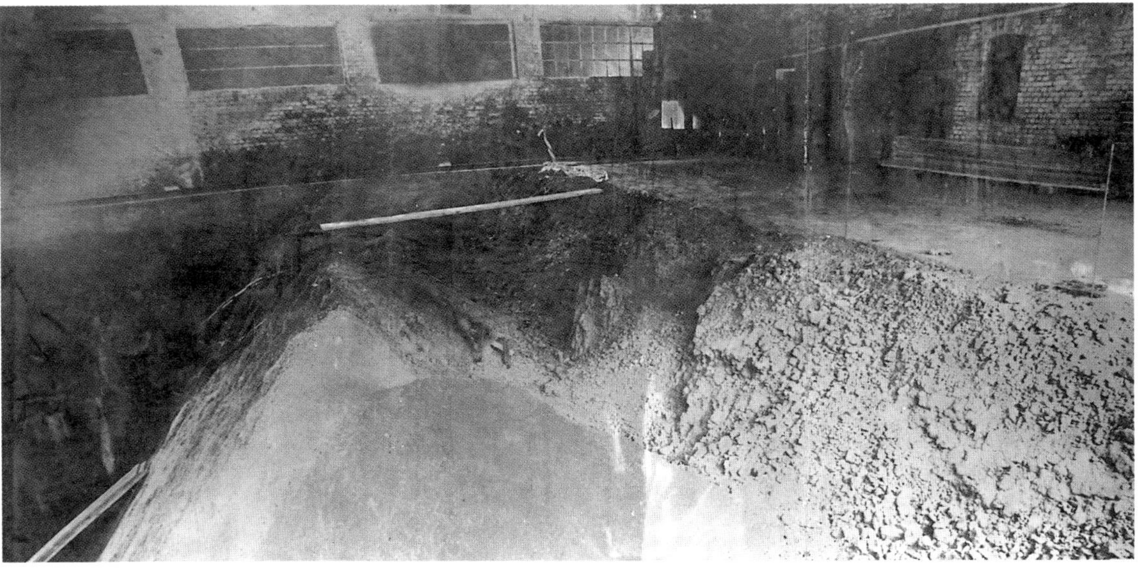

Anselm Kiefer *Die Himmelspälaste* (*The Heavenly Palaces*) (pages 4/5) 1990 ashes and acrylic on original photographs on cardboard 39 3/4 x 28 in. each page

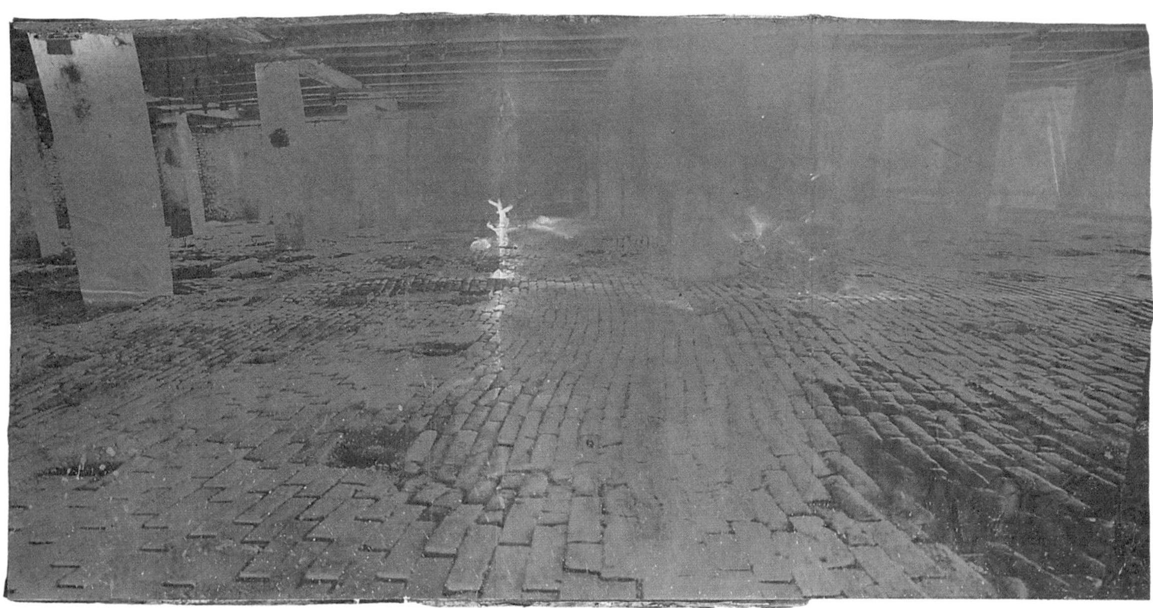

Anselm Kiefer *Die Himmelspäläste (The Heavenly Palaces)* (pages 6/7) 1990 ashes and acrylic on original photographs on cardboard 39 3/4 x 28 in. each page

Anselm Kiefer *Die Himmelspälaste* (*The Heavenly Palaces*) (pages 14/15) 1990 ashes and acrylic on original photographs on cardboard 39 3/4 x 28 in. each page

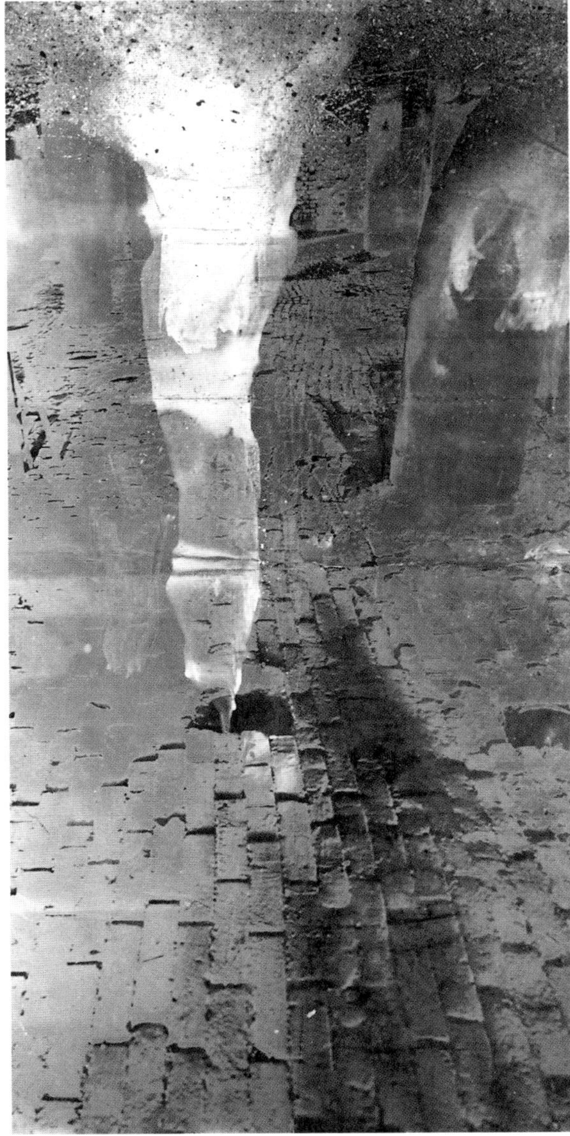

Anselm Kiefer *Die Himmelspälaste* (*The Heavenly Palaces*) (pages 18/19) 1990 ashes and acrylic on original photographs on cardboard 39 3/4 x 28 in each page

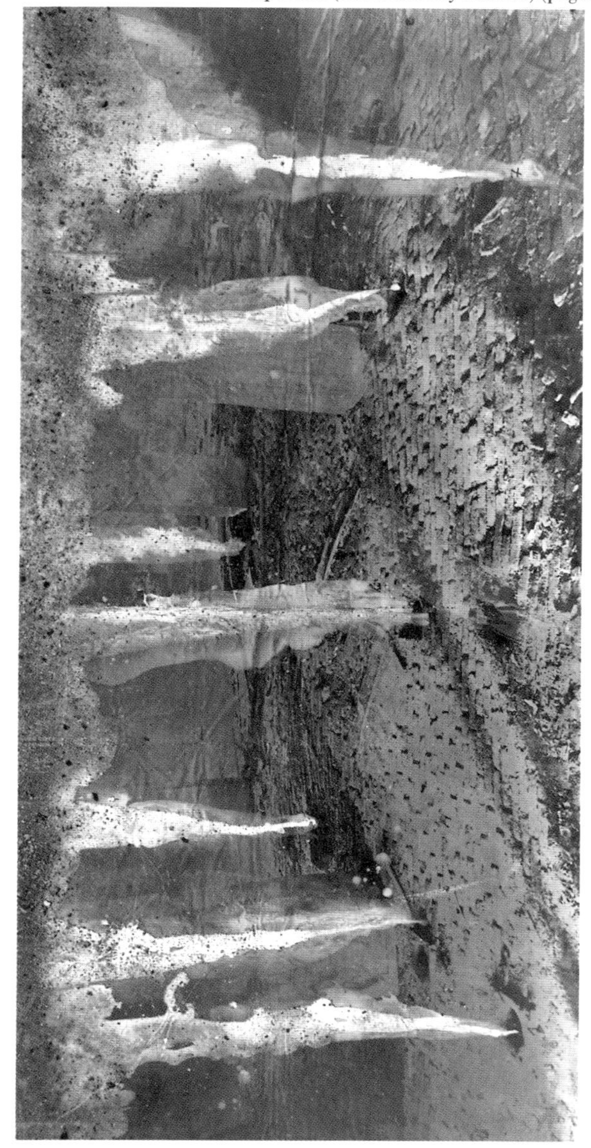

LOTHAR BAUMGARTEN

Since the early 1970s Lothar Baumgarten has explored the relationships between tribal cultures in South and North America and the peoples of European origins who have encroached upon or conquered and decimated these indigenous societies. In the course of this ongoing project, Baumgarten has traveled through the Americas, living for extended periods with native peoples; mounted museum and gallery installations; exhibited photographs; made films; written texts; and published books. Central to his work is his view of language and the power of naming as key in the ordering of experience and claiming of control over the environment and social relationships. He sees language as both a map and a weapon. Similarly for Baumgarten, photographs are another means for controlling perceptions and experiences, particularly in the way they reveal landscape as a record of human intervention in nature.

Baumgarten uses galleries and museums as points of focus for his work, as public arenas for inquiry into and recognition of suppressed meanings and histories. His installations often combine the painting and stenciling of names on walls. He sometimes juxtaposes words from a native language — for example, animal names — with words from a European language — for example, names of minerals — which for either culture, respectively, indicate how the environment is perceived and catalogued and how it can be used. Occasionally, Baumgarten uses mineral or plant materials for the pigment of his wall paintings — another abstraction derived from the natural environment. Photographs of the same landscape often are superimposed or hung alongside the words and wall painting. Overall, the works comprise an elegant and powerful passage through systems of signs — words, materials, images — that shapes our understanding of the environment, culture, and history.

Carbon, Baumgarten's most recent project, was begun in 1987. It has involved extensive train travel in the United States and residence on several Native American reservations. The title evokes the dark fuel made from the pressure of centuries' weight on organic materials. The work is a reflection on the palimpsest of Native American identity and landscape, names and places, which underlies contemporary

American life. Baumgarten's own description of the work, which follows, elucidates not only this particular inquiry but also gives insight into his general approach.

Carbon: A Demography of "Settling the West"

The subject and raw material of *Carbon* is the aroma of geography, as embodied in the names of the railroad lines covering this country. These names are polyphonic. They talk back to us about the confrontation of two multiple-shaped worlds: that of the continent's first inhabitants and that of the pioneer migrants to the West. On the one hand the names reflect the movement of a territorial expansion, the natural destination of which was the Pacific Ocean; on the other they testify to an older stratum, that of the Indian populations, their rivers and mountains, fords and trails. The linguistic blend of these names signifies the superimpositions of heterogeneous cultural strands.

The confrontation of the two worlds, accelerated by the advance of the rail, was generally not a harmonious one; the local cultures not confined to reservations were, more often than not, exterminated. As the land was gradually cleared of its native people, the westbound settlers claimed it as their own agricultural soil; private entrepreneurs followed suit and built the largest railroad system in the world, employing Chinese immigrants, men of yet a third continent, as their welcome manpower.

Prerequisite to the development of the newly acquired lands, an impressive fabric of tracks and sophisticated bridges was thus woven, built upon the pillars of red expropriation and yellow exploitation. The railroad covered a continent of miraculously diverse landscapes, animals, and plants — some of them changed, cultivated, or destroyed, some preserved as they were before the coming of the white man. Encompassing the rail network and its environs, this diversity of peoples, history, and landscape has been the constant companion of the enchanted rail traveler through the years.

For a time I became such a traveler. I sensed what it is like to live in a nation steadily on the move. *Carbon* connotes the confrontations of cultures that have been a part of this movement and development through an artistic grammar that engages the particular geographic and architectural contexts of its site. [1]

1 Baumgarten wrote this description in 1989. It is reprinted here with his permission.

Lothar Baumgarten *Carbon* 1987–1990 (detail) wall painting Installation view, Museum of Contemporary Art, Los Angeles

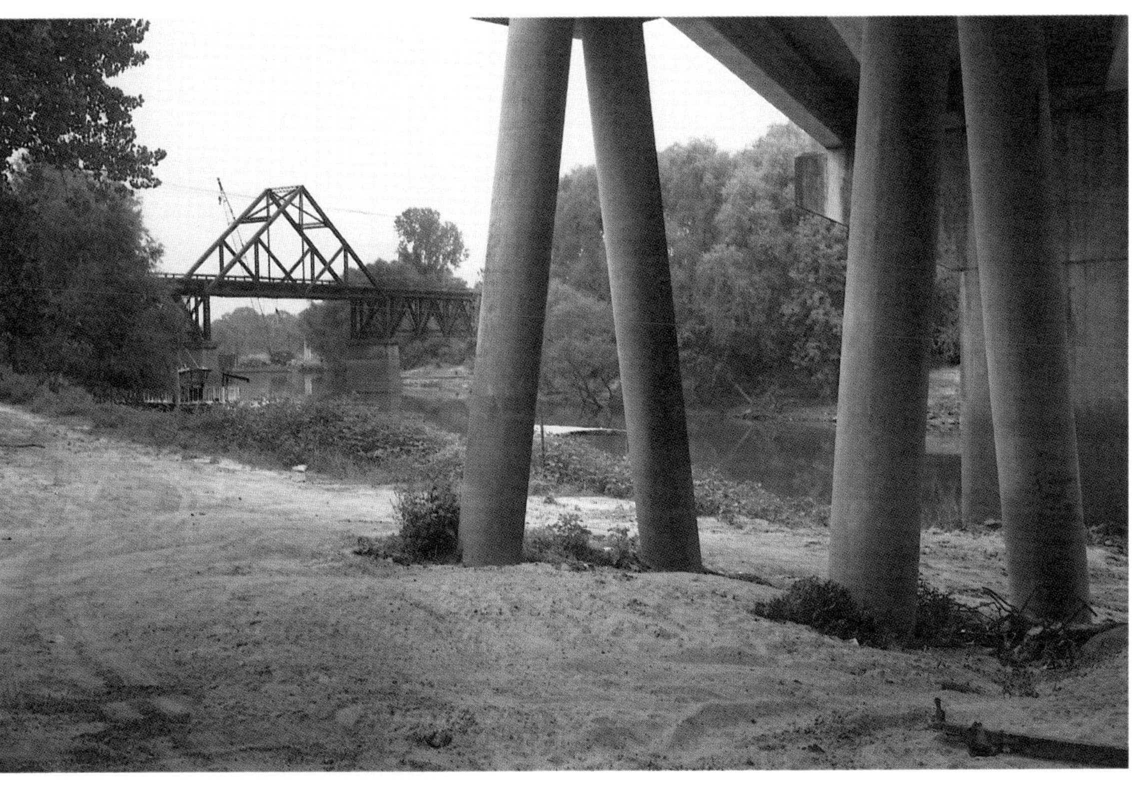

Lothar Baumgarten *Texas & Pacific Railway, Triangle bridge truss, Twelve-mile Bayou, Shreveport, Caddo County, Louisiana* 1989 gelatin silver print 15 1/4 x 22 1/2 in.

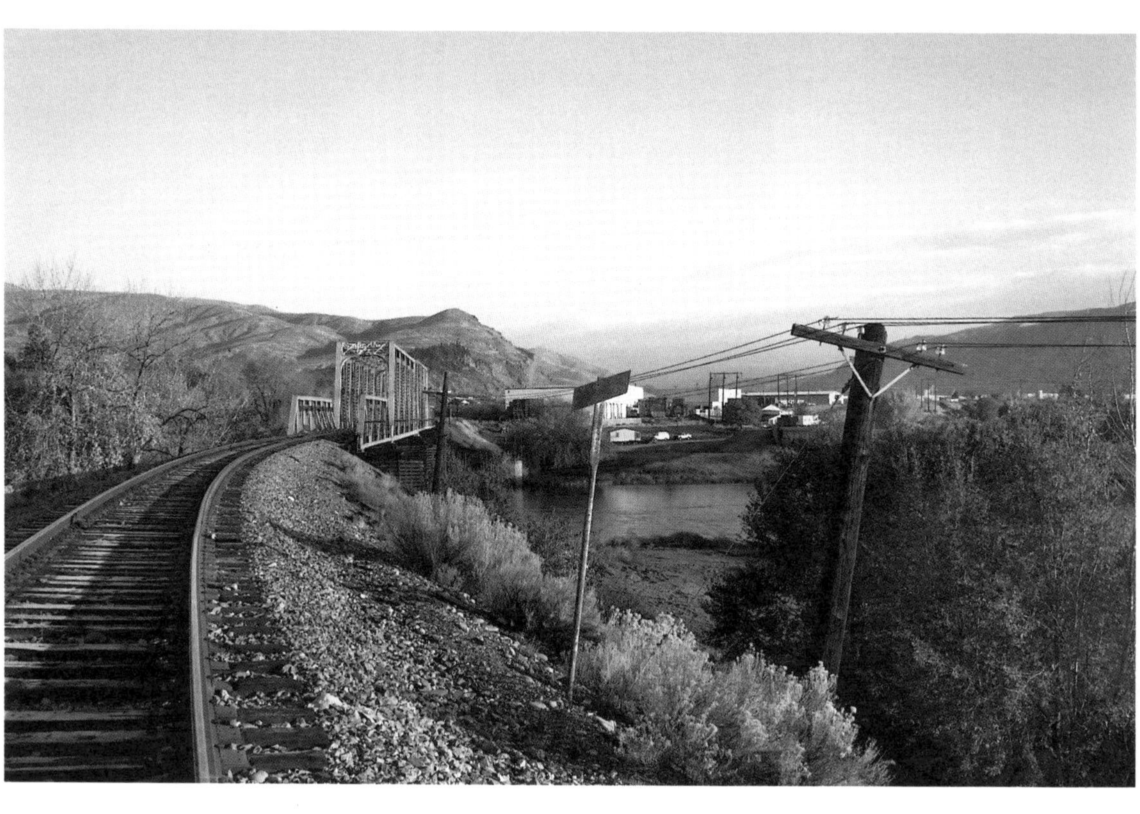

Lothar Baumgarten *Burlington Northern Railroad, Warren through truss bridge, Columbia River, Wenatchee, Celan County, Washington* 1989 gelatin silver print 15 1/4 x 22 1/2 in.

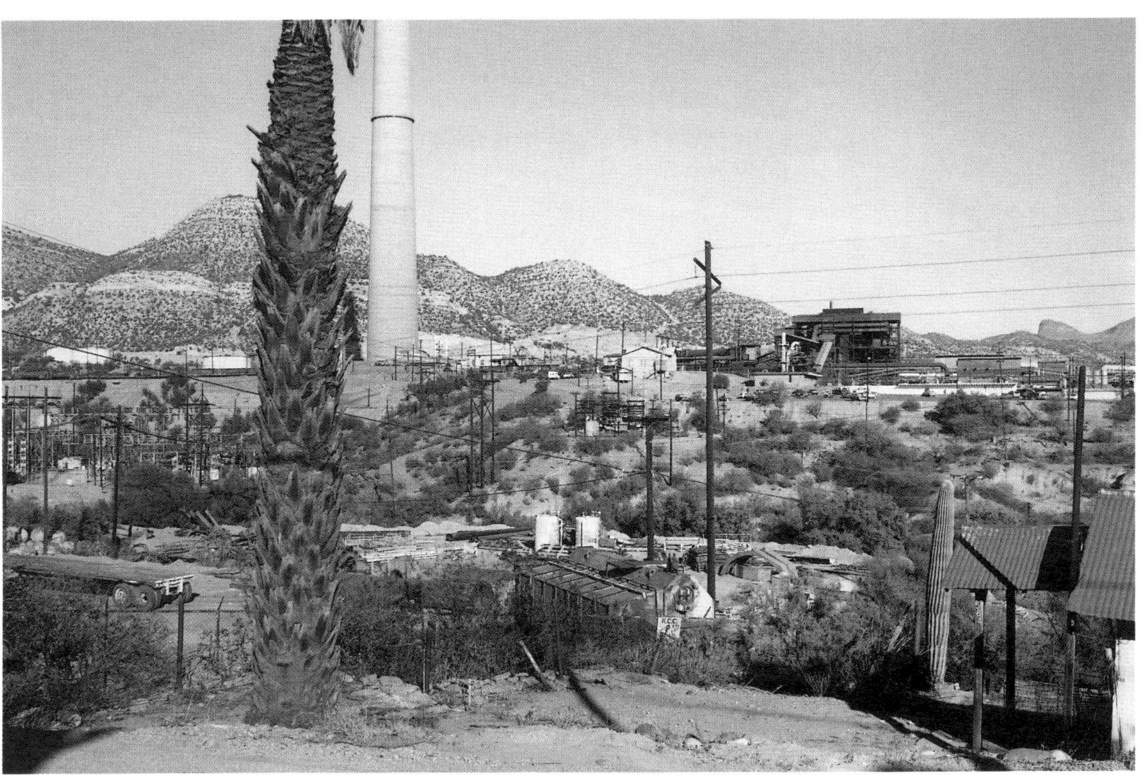

Lothar Baumgarten *Copper mine, Hayden, Pinal County, Arizona* 1989 gelatin silver print 15 1/4 x 22 1/2 in.

BERNHARD AND ANNA BLUME

Bernhard and Anna Blume have worked as a husband-and-wife team since 1980. Prior to that, Bernhard Blume made photographic works alone. He was a student of Joseph Beuys at the Düsseldorf art academy, and Beuys' influence is apparent. Like Beuys, the Blumes stage performances with themselves as the subjects. Unlike Beuys, however, these actions are not intended for an audience but are strictly for the camera. They act out stories, seemingly absurd narratives and situations, in which the prosaic details of middle-class life and everyday reality are thrown into disarray. The photographs are blown up to an enormous scale, printed in black-and-white, and presented in multipart sequences. In character they are somewhat akin to American vaudeville and slapstick comedy, but their subjects are usually specific to German life and culture. Even without being able to appreciate the many references, any audience can respond to the exaggerated humor of these photographs. Along with the large-scale black-and-white works, the Blumes also have been taking Polaroids, from which they make small, brilliantly colored collages, more like absurd still lifes than stories, but in which they continue their central role as subjects.

Bernhard Blume also has studied and taught philosophy. His photographic works reflect his pursuit of philosophical subjects such as the nature of truth and how it is perceived, the various conditions of being, and the existential meanings of life. The camera has become as much of a tool as language in exploring these subjects, so that although the photographs may initially appear to be only farcical melodramas, they mask an underlying seriousness of intent and inquiry. An early photograph, *Demonstrative Identifikation mit dem ALL = Magischer Subjektivismus* (*Demonstrative Identification with the Universal = Magical Subjectivism*) (1971), provides a key to understanding the more serious side of the Blumes' work. It also places their images historically as a response to Subjective Photography, the movement that dominated the production of photographic images as art in Germany in the 1950s. This movement, whose prime exemplar was Otto Steinert, explored the photographic image as a means to express individual inner states of feeling and consciousness. The Blumes, in contrast, use photography as a means of throwing open to question the nature of knowledge and the ways in which beliefs are socially determined.

Bernhard Blume has written extensively on his philosophy about his work:

"I use the mechanism of the camera, developed to produce supposedly objective representations of the visible world, in a critical way — as a means of critically examining our epistemological assumptions. That means my use of it is subjective!"[1]

"The body as a whole is incorporated into the system of symbolic rituals which determine social roles and mark acceptance into the community. But to our isolated consciousness, in its fixation on words and images, society appears as an abstract entity, in contrast to our apparent freedom. But our role in society is just as completely determined. It is equally ritualised and even more strongly internalised, but is characterised by a neurotic neglect of the body. Yet in the photos at least we seem to have been physically present. And the photos prove it."[2]

For the works included in this exhibition, *Metaphysik ist Männersache* aus der Serie Im Wald (*Metaphysics Is Man's Business* from the series In the Forest) (1991), the Blumes staged a series of photographs in the Black Forest. The images reflect an uneasy relationship between figures and trees; communion between man and nature is disrupted — a scenario that undercuts the vital mystical and mythical role of the forest in German culture. The belief that, in going back to the forest, one can commune with nature and find the truth about oneself and the world has been a persistent theme in German art, literature, and philosophy. This belief is, of course, part of the legacy of Romanticism throughout the Western world. A more generalized version of this thinking has long been at play in American culture, as many social movements have sought salvation and a heightening of consciousness through a return to nature. Blind faith, the Blumes seem to imply, is an inadequate response to a world in which rationalized behavior controls social outcomes. The death of forests in Germany and throughout the industrialized world in the late twentieth century stems from such behavior and from man's hubristic drive to triumph over nature. Any effective counteraction to this pervasive social tendency requires a critical rather than a mystical response. The Blumes engage an audience through their entertainment but then provide a twist to their own moral tale with their implication that we, too, must take seriously our roles in our own dramas.

1 Statement by Bernhard Blume in *Behind the Eyes: Eight German Artists*, exh. cat. (San Francisco Museum of Modern Art, 1986), p. 127.

2 Ibid., p. 126.

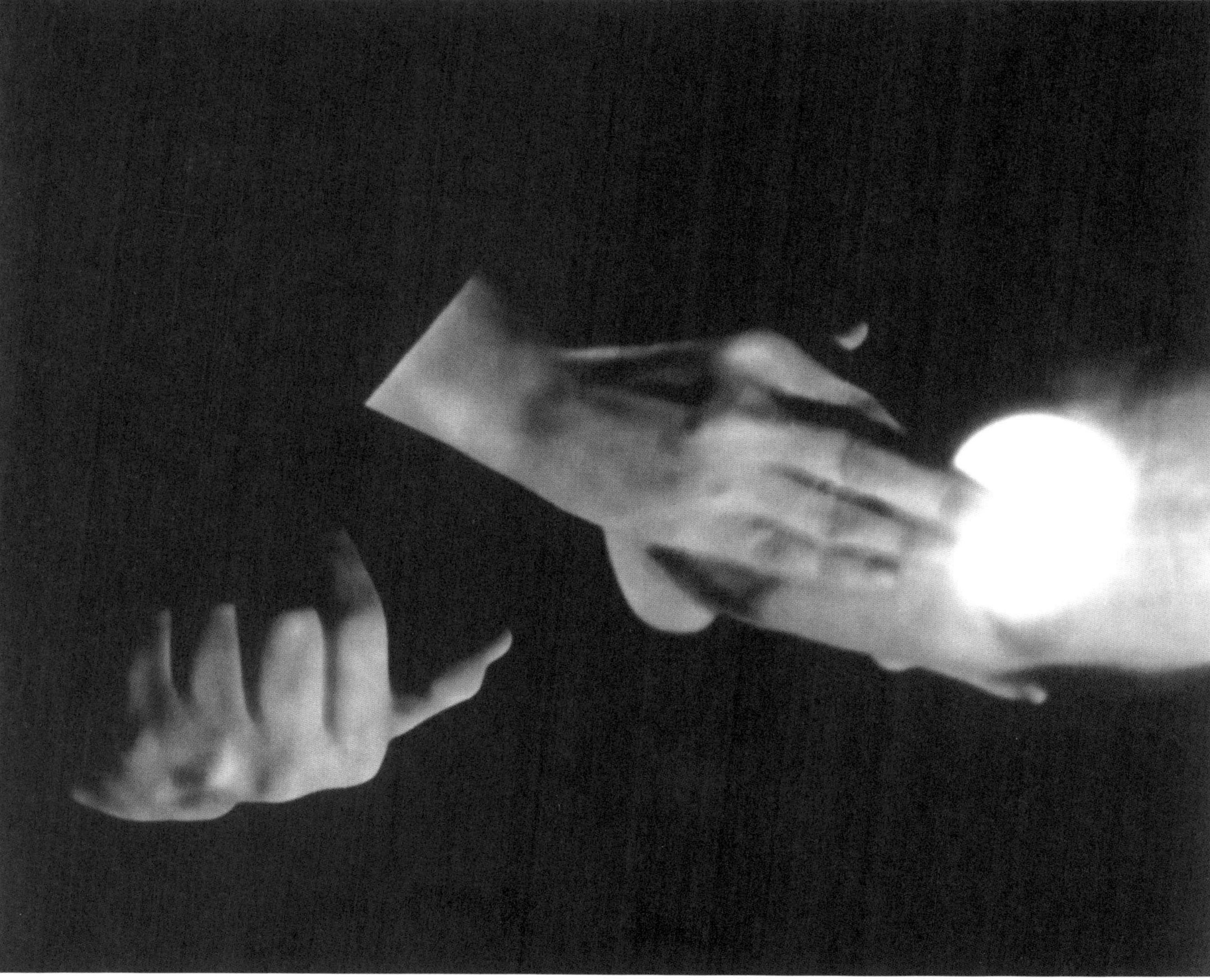

Bernhard Johannes Blume *Demonstrative Identifikation mit dem ALL = Magischer Subjektivismus (Demonstrative Identification with the Universal = Magical Subjectivism)* 1971
black-and-white photograph 23 5/8 x 19 11/16 in.

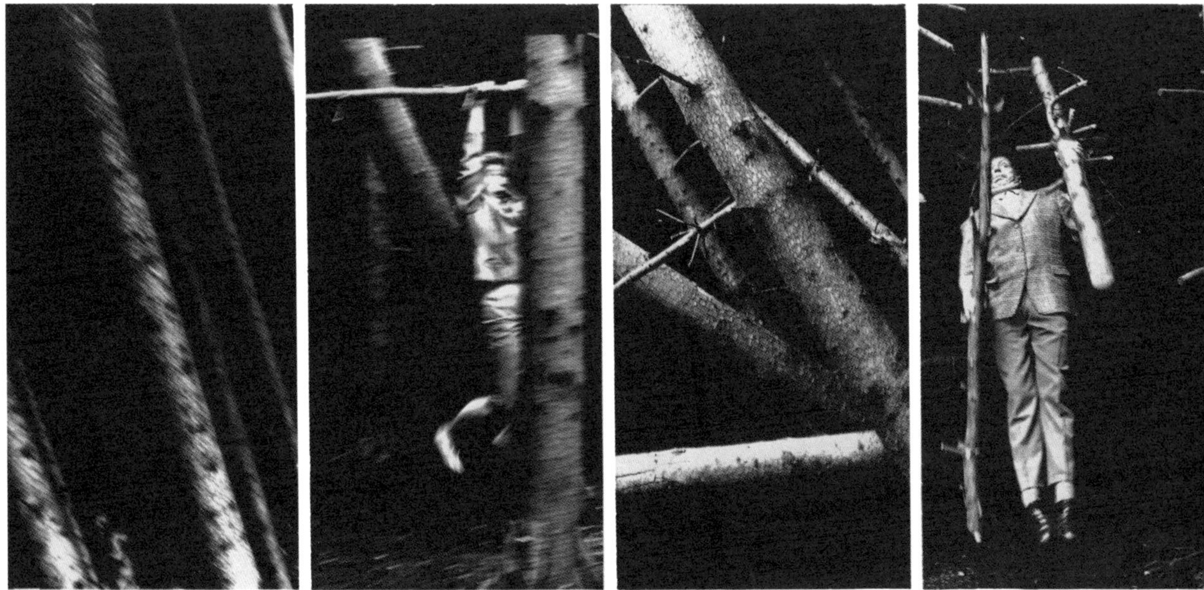

Anna and Bernhard Blume *Metaphysik ist Männersache* aus der Serie Im Wald (*Metaphysics Is Man's Business* from the series In the Forest) 1991 seven black-and-white photographs 98 1/2 x 49 3/4 in. each

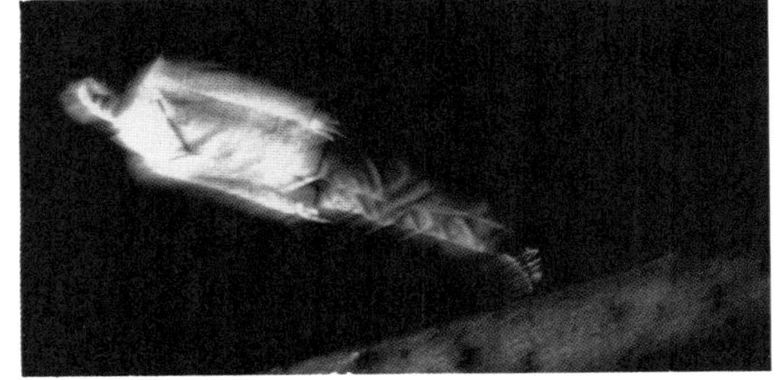

KATHARINA SIEVERDING

Like many of the German artists who came into their own in the late 1960s and early 1970s, Katharina Sieverding was a student of Joseph Beuys. His preoccupation with controlling the persona — the fabricated public personality — of the artist, and his sense of the artist as social actor was readily adopted by Sieverding. Her first works were extended series of self-portraits, her face filling the frame, close to the lens, eyes staring directly into the camera and, by implication, out at the viewer. By changing light, shifting focus, and altering her makeup, she created a phantasmagoric series of characters — relentless, confrontational, and frightening but also seductive and vulnerable. She has attempted to isolate psychic states outside of social and cultural frames or historical identifications. The resulting images are portraits of female personality hidden by masks that cannot be removed. They are always controlled, contrived images of interior states, produced for effect.

In the mid-1970s Sieverding began making enormous photographic tableaux, combining images and text, in which she occasionally appeared as a character. This work grew increasingly sophisticated, both in its seamless fusion of pictures and captions and in its social commentary, which was influenced by her travels in 1976 and 1977 to the United States and, in 1978, to China. In the United States, billboards are used for advertising, largely to promote commercial products; in China they are used to expound political ideology and the idolization of the political leadership. In both cases, these large displays in public places are used to encourage identification with the image, to absorb the private individual into a social frame. Sieverding's works of this period engage questions of social politics: To what extent is an individual free of or controlled by society? Who is the actor, and who is the victim? Where are the lines drawn between private and social responsibility and between personal and political power? In a work included in this exhibition, *Unwiderstehliche historische Strömung* (*Irresistible Historical Current*) (1979), the actor in the drama appears isolated and caught by some abstract force. The caption freezes the narrative and projects a social meaning onto the image. The overall effect is both confrontational and ambiguous, and there is present as well a lurking sense of danger and uneasiness. As a woman in an art world dominated by men and as a German in a political world dominated by jousting superpowers, Sieverding captures the fright and the privilege of the marginalized voyeur.

In her work of the past decade, Sieverding has returned to self-portraiture, making several series. The portraits of the early 1980s are cool and stylized, distant and aloof; they show figures of a demimonde inhabiting a world of darkness. The faces are masked by makeup and brought out of the darkness by colored light, recalling visions of the Berlin cabarets between the world wars. More recent portraits, such as *Die Sonne um Mitternacht schauen* (*To Look at the Sun at Midnight*) (1988) in this exhibition, recall her work of the late 1960s and early 1970s, with the face again abstracted and filling the frame. Rather than being isolated images, the faces now have been fused into strips, reducing the individuality of each portrait. They are combined into enormous overall compositions of black, red, and gold, seeming about to melt under a solar flare. While the portraits of the early 1980s are like film stills, the late portraits resemble filmstrips.

In addition to the self-portraits, Sieverding has continued to create huge photographic compositions that display firestorms, mass rituals, and media icons. They are much more abstract than the earlier billboardlike photographs. In both the large, composite, late self-portraits and in the hieratic tableaux, the scenes are hallucinogenic; an eerie, piercing view into spectral darkness is granted by a release of light. Some reckoning with history, apocalypse, salvation, or damnation seems at hand. The fates of the individual and of society have been joined.

The recognition of the photograph as a literal and symbolic fusion of light and darkness is at the heart of Sieverding's work. She understands the particular propensity of the photographic image to exploit the boundaries between exposing and fabricating a sense of reality, a quality manipulated masterfully in both advertising and film — two media that have strongly influenced her. In a unique way she has used the photographic image for expressive and visionary ends.

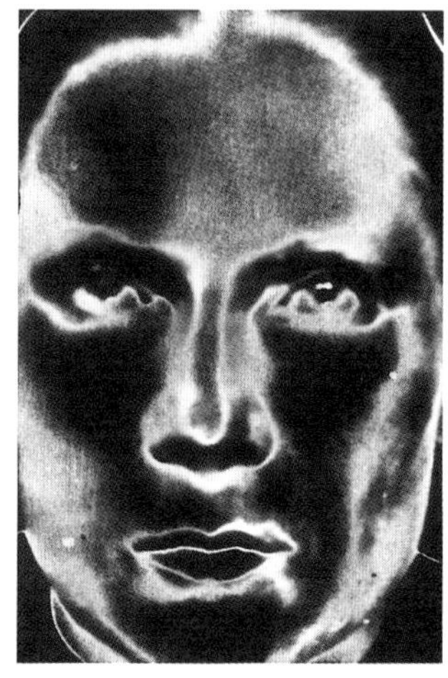

Katharina Sieverding photograph from *MATON V* 1969 twenty black-and-white photographs 27 1/2 x 19 3/4 in. each

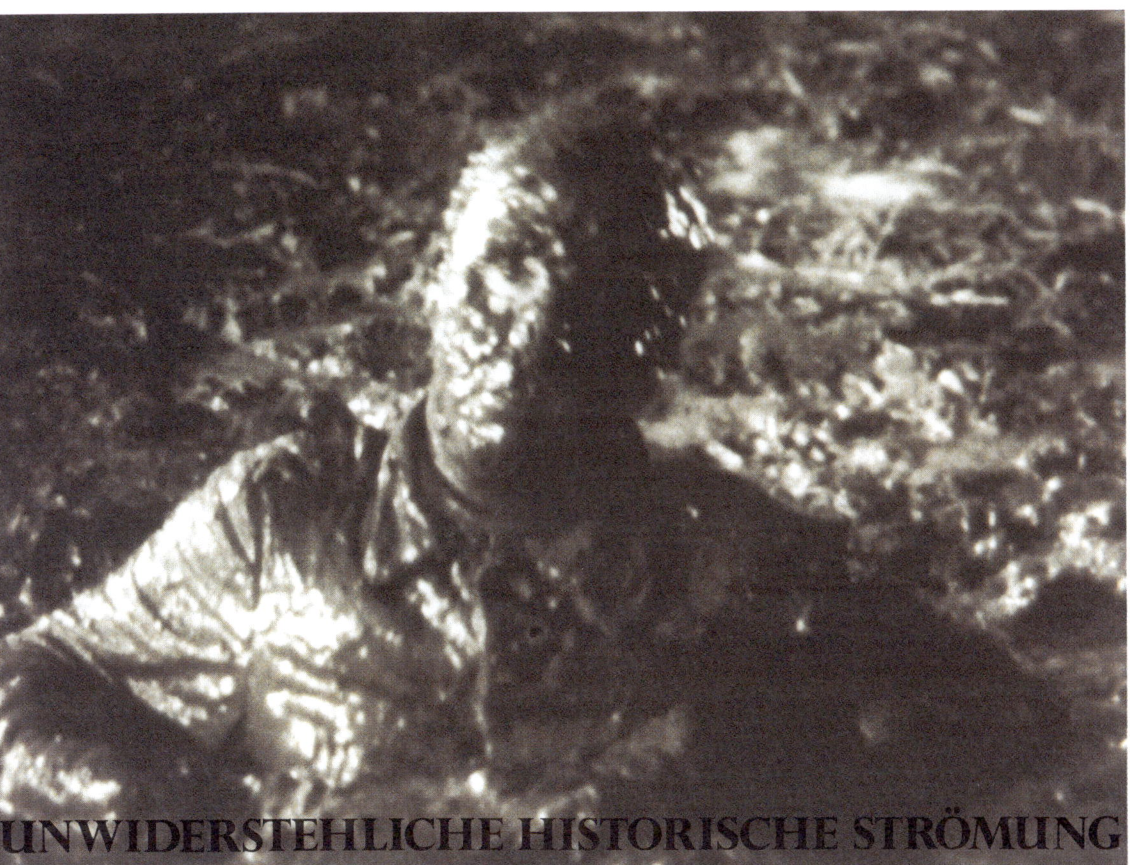

Katharina Sieverding *Unwiderstehliche historiche Strömung (Irresistible Historical Current)* 1979 three color photographs, acrylic, steel 118 x 147 in. overall

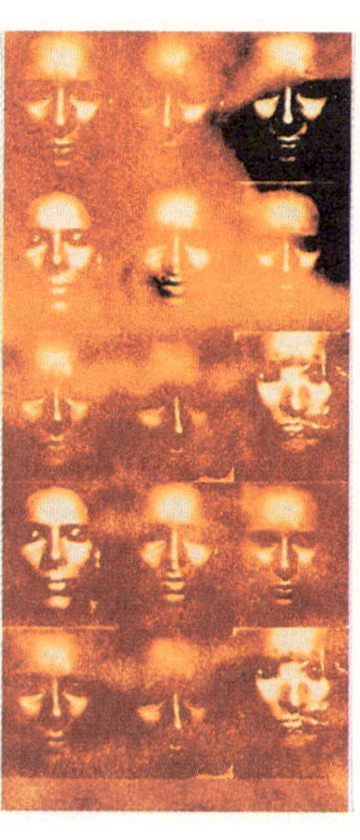
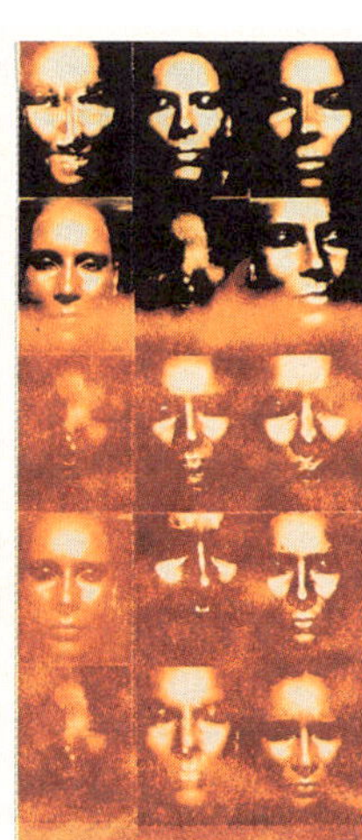
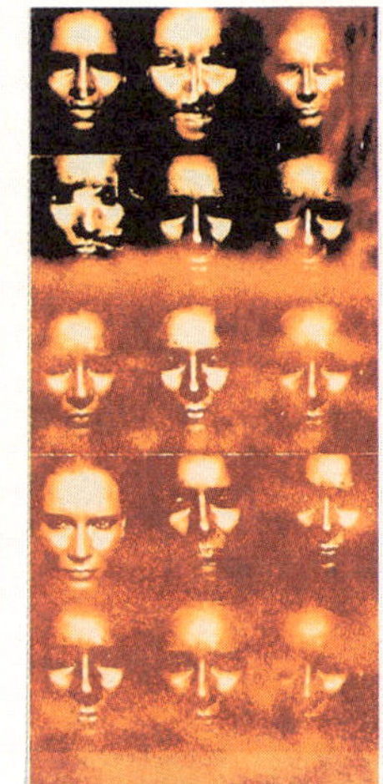
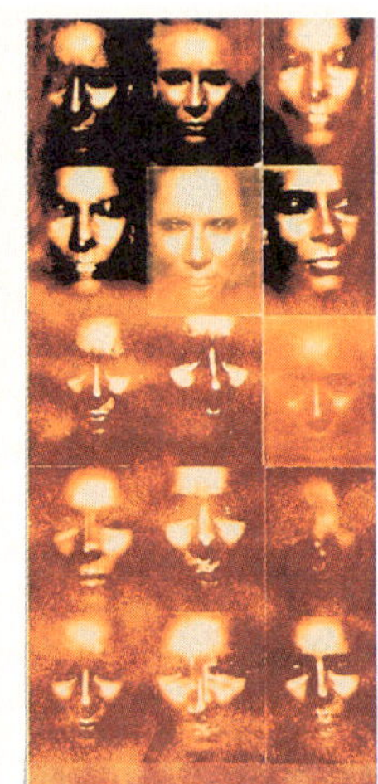
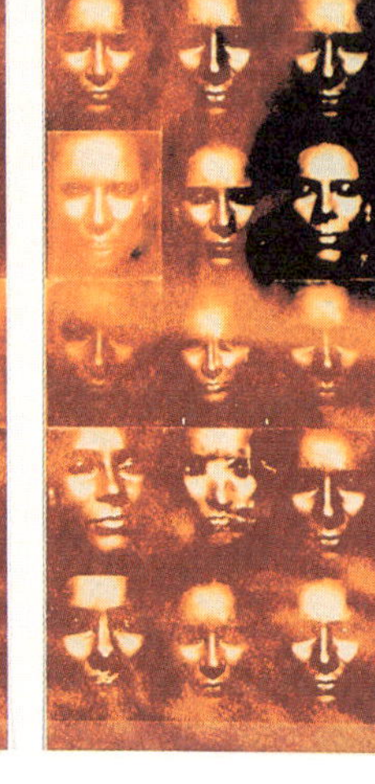

Katharina Sieverding *Die Sonne um Mitternacht schauen (To Look at the Sun at Midnight)* 1988 five color photographs, acrylic, steel 108 x 256 in. overall

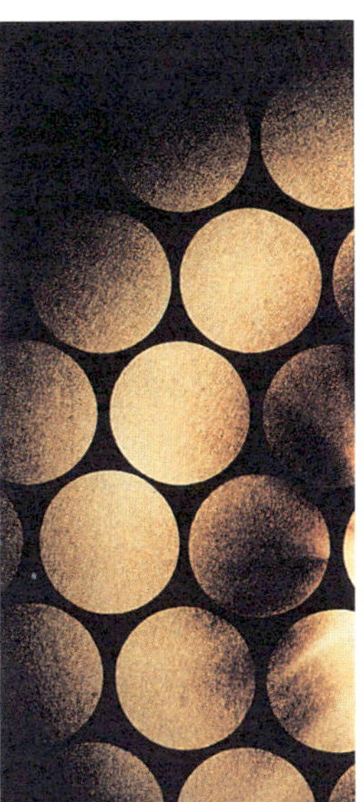
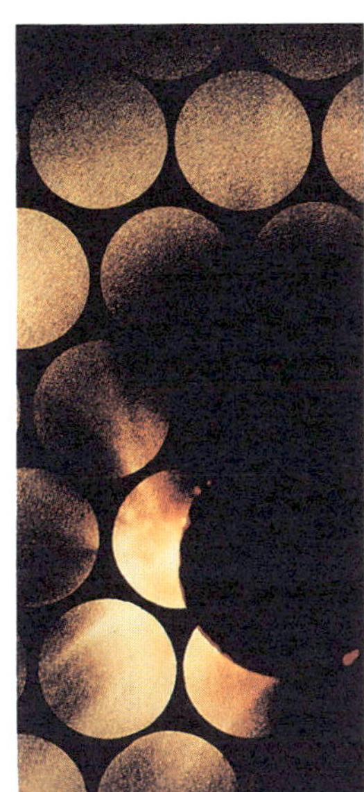
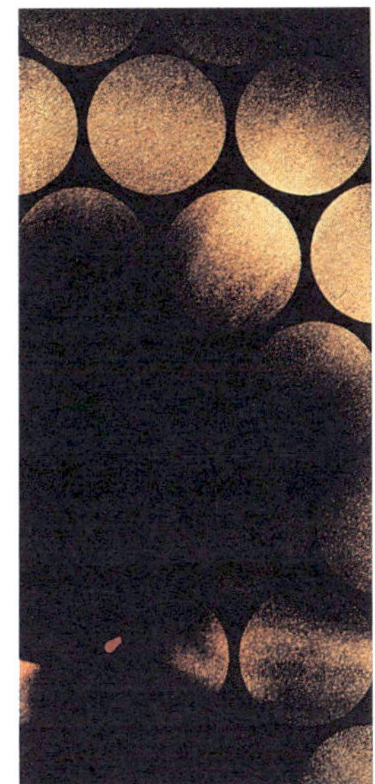
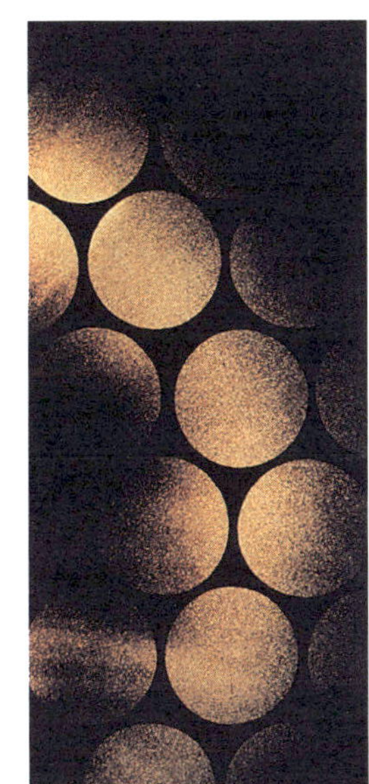

Katharina Sieverding *Kontinentalkern XL, Sonne, die Erde imprägnierend (Continental Core, Sun, Impregnating the Earth)* 1990 four color photographs, acrylic, steel 108 1/4 x 208 5/8 in. overall

ASTRID KLEIN

Astrid Klein began working in the mid-1970s, using images taken from the media to make very large newspaperlike photographs with captions superimposed. The influence of the work of Katharina Sieverding was important for her in this period. Klein's early images had strong political overtones, dealing with rebellion and victimization and journalistic exploitation. Through the last decade, however, Klein's work has become more introspective and psychological. Without relinquishing its probing, critical questioning of the relationship between individuals and society, her work has grown more abstract and elegiac.

Since the mid-1980s, Klein has made large-scale black-and-white photographs, frequently and closely integrating images and language. The figurative references in them sometimes are highly manipulated and often difficult to identify, ambiguous as to what they might represent and as to the sources from which they derive. The images appear as dreamlike apparitions and epiphanies. Words float into or across the images as almost godlike invocations — the apocryphal handwriting on the wall. The photographs are read as signs into a hidden world. They are experienced as psychological states of being.

Klein's more recent work continues an important stream of photographically based art in Germany, beginning with the Bauhaus experiments of the 1920s, in which manipulation of the negative and of the printing process allowed a new depth of subjective expression in the image. Klein, however, takes the processes and effects developed in Bauhaus photography to new extremes of manipulation and scale. The curator Jean-Pierre LeGrand writes, "She subjects the negatives, made from images taken from the media, to mechanical and chemical transformation processes; she draws, makes sketches, superimposes networks and grids; she enlarges, splits, makes photomontages, double exposures and combinations of positive and negative images, in an art that has as much to do with light as with the negative, since, as a result of the reversal in printing, what is hidden in the negative becomes clear in the print."[1]

In *Verführung – Sklaverei* (*Seduction – Slavery*), a series of five photographs completed in 1988, Klein composed a visual structure to correspond to deep subconscious fears and promises. The elegant beauty of these photographs is both delectable and terrifying, with shimmering whites and glowing blacks, suspended forms appearing with encrusted, jewellike surfaces. Space in the photographs seems both architectural, like prisons or monuments, and organic — capable of melting like ice, erupting into fire, or dissolving like clouds. It is simultaneously urban and primordial. Etched into the images are the words *seduction* and *slavery* in German and, in one case, in Greek. The final image contains the Greek word *tamoé*, meaning utopia, and is taken from the title of a story by the Marquis de Sade about his utopian vision. The works seem to ask whether freedom is to be found in the cutting of bonds and unshackling of chains, or whether it is a condition in which there is nothing to be lost. They seem to ask to what degree society is a reflection of the aggregate of human fears and desires.

Klein's work shares a feminist edge with that of many other contemporary women artists. However, she avoids taking a political, didactic, or propagandistic stance. Instead, she exposes dark psychological associations that stem from both the inner world of the mind and its social frame. The states of consciousness she explores are equally primal, unchanging conditions of the human psyche, and contingent — products of social conventions and conditioning. History is seen as an apparition, an overlay, a construction in which the mind in its pure state must exist, function, and perform.

1 Quoted from LeGrand's entry on Klein in *Blickpunkte*, exh. cat., trans. Susan Le Pan (Montreal: Musée d'Art Contemporain de Montreal, 1989), p. 73.

Astrid Klein *Verführung – Sklaverei III* (*Seduction – Slavery III*) 1988 black-and-white photograph 77 1/2 x 46 5/8 in.

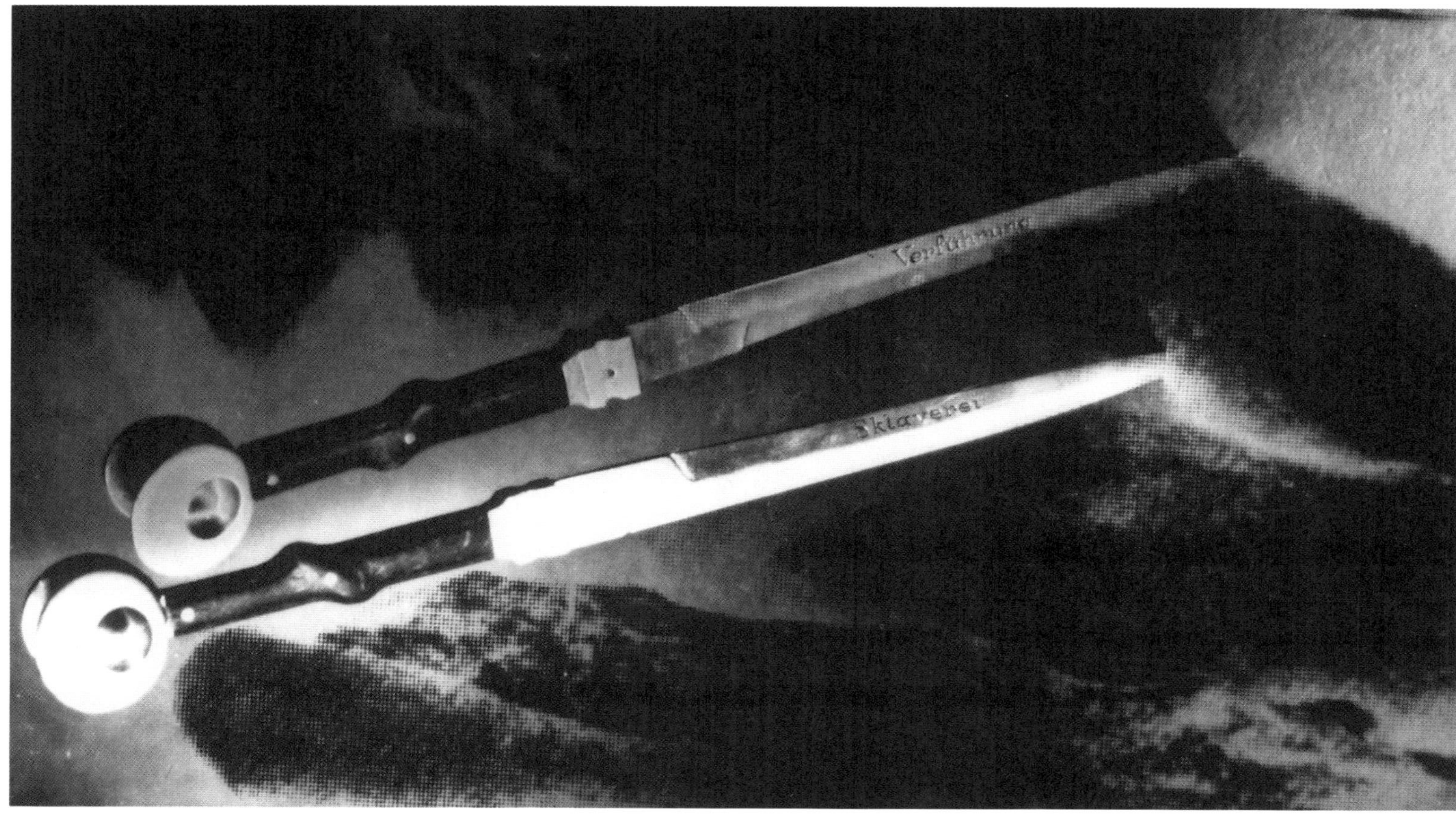

Astrid Klein *Verführung – Sklaverei V* (*Seduction – Slavery V*) 1988 black-and-white photograph 77 x 51 in.

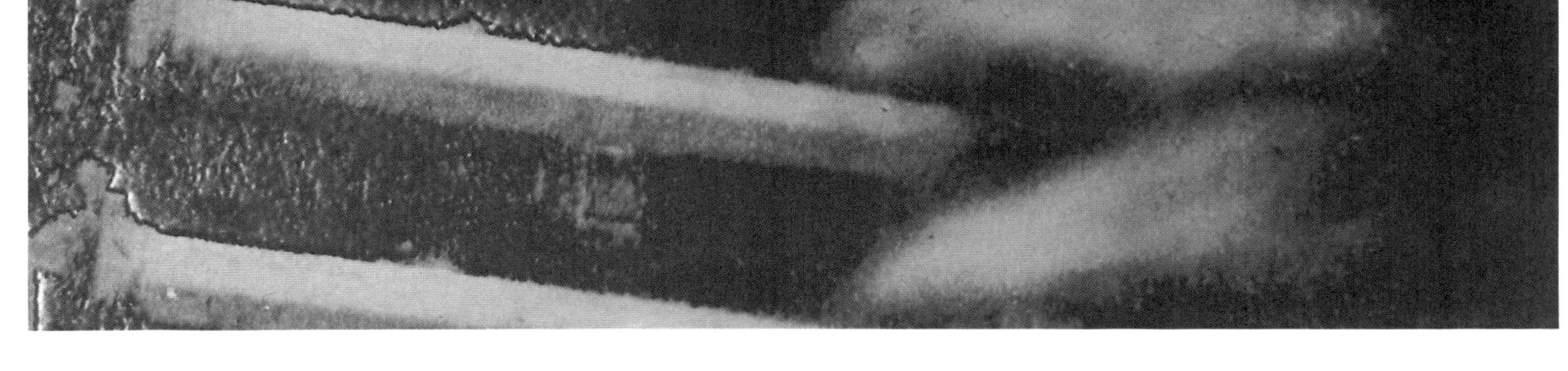

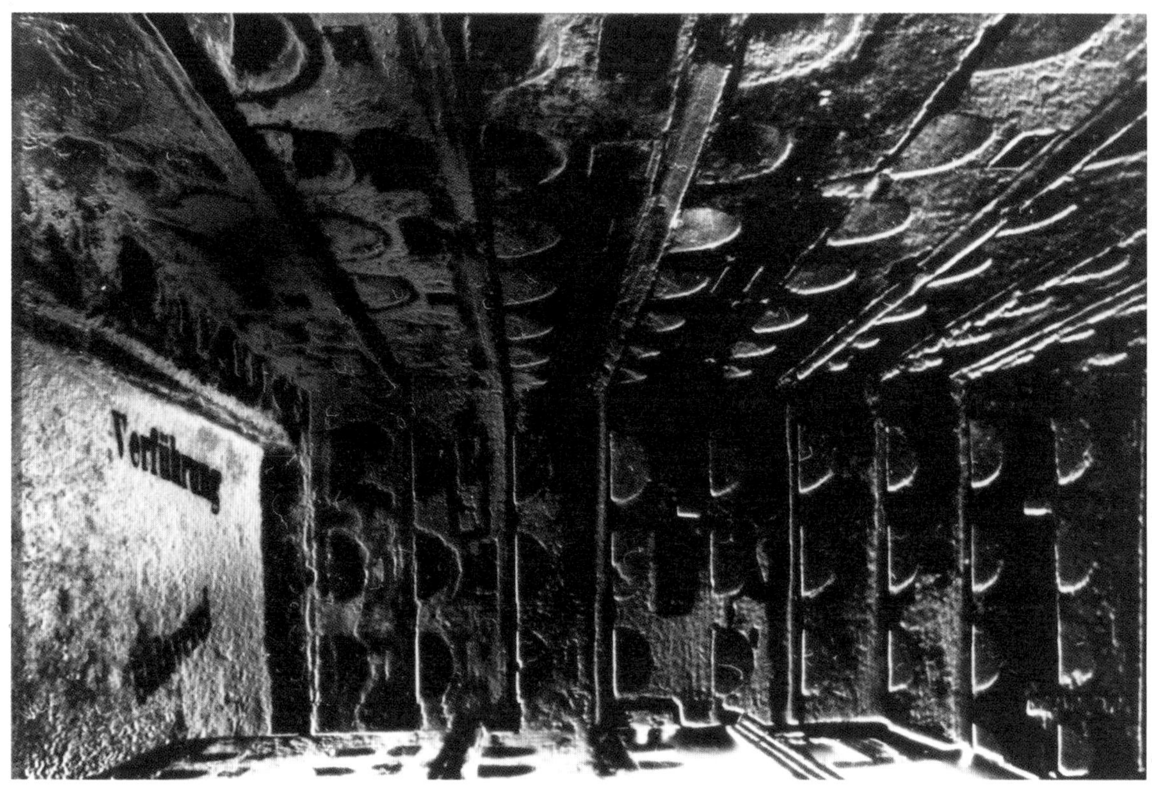

Astrid Klein *Verführung – Sklaverei I* (*Seduction – Slavery I*) 1988 black-and-white photograph 51 x 76 1/4 in.

MARTIN KIPPENBERGER

Martin Kippenberger established himself in the 1980s as the enfant terrible of the contemporary German art world: he is prankster-hipster, self-conscious-unselfconscious, punk and player — a kind of Dadaist commando. His work is irreverent, mocking of self and society and filled with puns and in-jokes on the art world. It can be wildly imaginative and humorous, as well as blatantly distasteful and offensive. Influenced by both Joseph Beuys and Sigmar Polke, Kippenberger moves incessantly between media. He has made installations, filling rooms with a wide assortment of materials, as well as discrete assemblages and constructions. He works as often making books and drawings as he does making sculptural objects. It is not surprising that photography has entered his work at different times and in various forms.

Recently, Kippenberger made a large group of works collectively entitled *Heavy Mädel* (1989 – 1990) — an allusion to "heavy metal" and to the anarchic but fashionable world of rock bands. *Mädel* translates literally in German dialect to mean *girl*, adding a layer of sexual reference. The identification with rock is a reflection of his perception of the artist as both entertainer and "art star" and of his own work as dissident, operating by his own rules, both energetic and forceful. *Heavy Mädel* is one example of Kippenberger's overloaded collage aesthetic, in which he layers both materials and references by language and allusion.

These new works began as paintings of collages made from posters, catalogues, and exhibition-invitation cards. They were made in various sizes, small and large, with colorful, textured overlays of images and language. Of the paintings, the question is which, if any, were executed by Kippenberger. Probably, all of them were produced by an assistant who knew how to make a "Kippenberger." Fastened onto the surfaces of these paintings were molded acrylic toys, into which Kippenberger (or someone) melted one or more cigarette butts. *Kippen* in German means to dump rubbish and is the colloquial expression for cigarette butts; *berg* is a mountain or hill or the peak of a curve. He thus attached his signature to the paintings, again a more literal add-on rather than a mere artistic autograph.

After being fabricated, the paintings were photographed, and after that, mirror-image drawings were made of the photographs. This reversal in the drawings refers to the inner workings of the photographic process, in which the lens inverts and turns the image upside down inside the camera. Once the drawings were completed, the paintings were destroyed. Thus the works now exist only as photographs and not as paintings. This, too, is a play on the fact that most works of art are better known as photographic reproductions than in their original form. In Kippenberger's logic, why not keep the potential for reproduction "true" to the originals — that is, to the photographs?

Kippenberger catches the slippery character of contemporary urban life, with its various levels of removal from direct experience, its fabricated and synthetic materials and cultural overlays and products. A materialist culture, it is fed by and consumes a glut of images, which this artist takes as his raw material. He celebrates the energy of this life but realizes its potential for a nasty hangover. His art has the capacity to be insulting and insensitive. But just as Kippenberger readily lampoons "good" social character, he is also more than willing to be the "butt" of his own jokes. While his work is carefully self-conscious, the most important aspect of it is the way it represents the spontaneity and immediacy of everyday life, in which the camera is the ever-ready, ubiquitous tool for making and reproducing images.

Martin Kippenberger *Untitled* 1989–1990 color photograph 35 1/2 x 29 1/2 in.

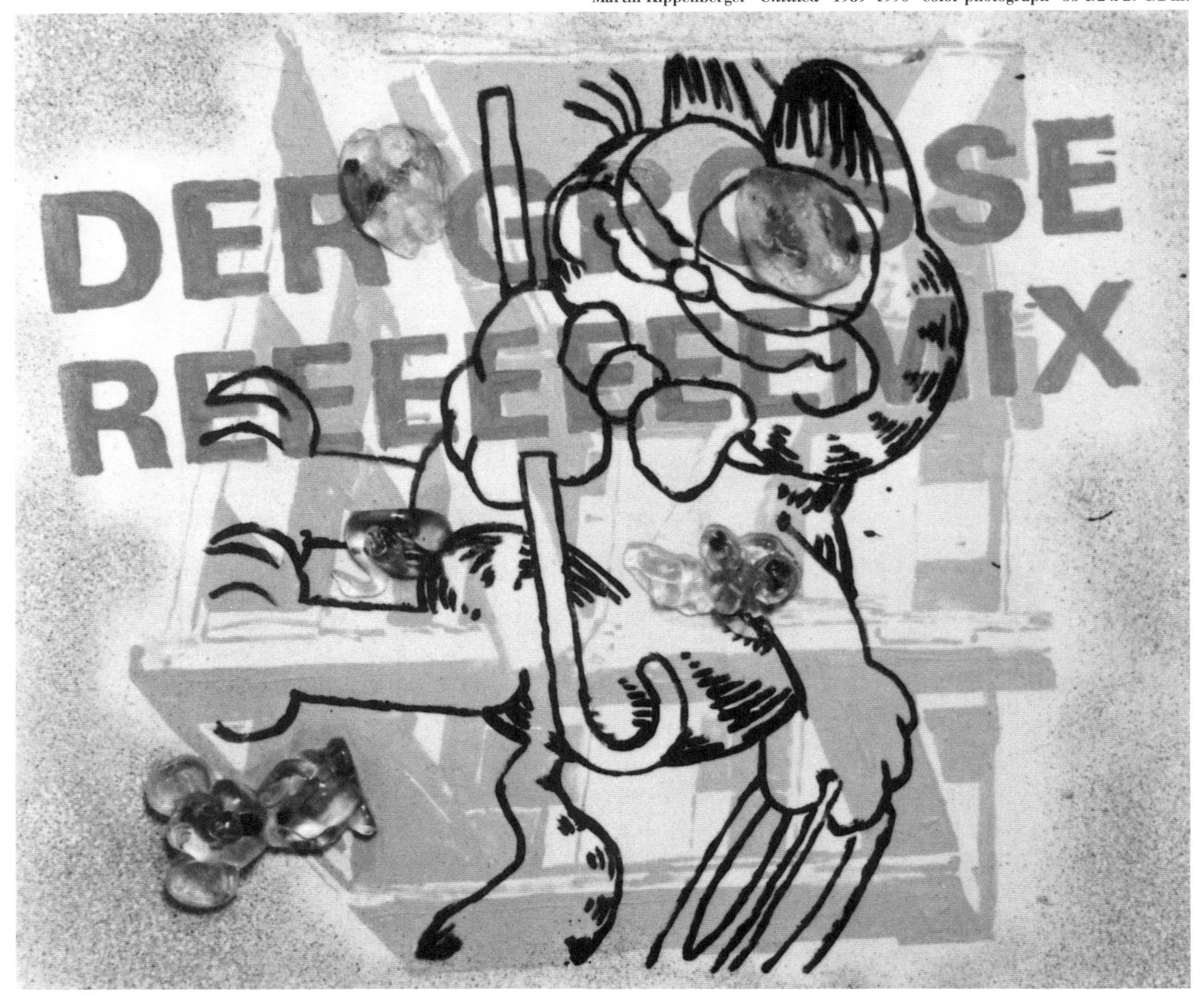

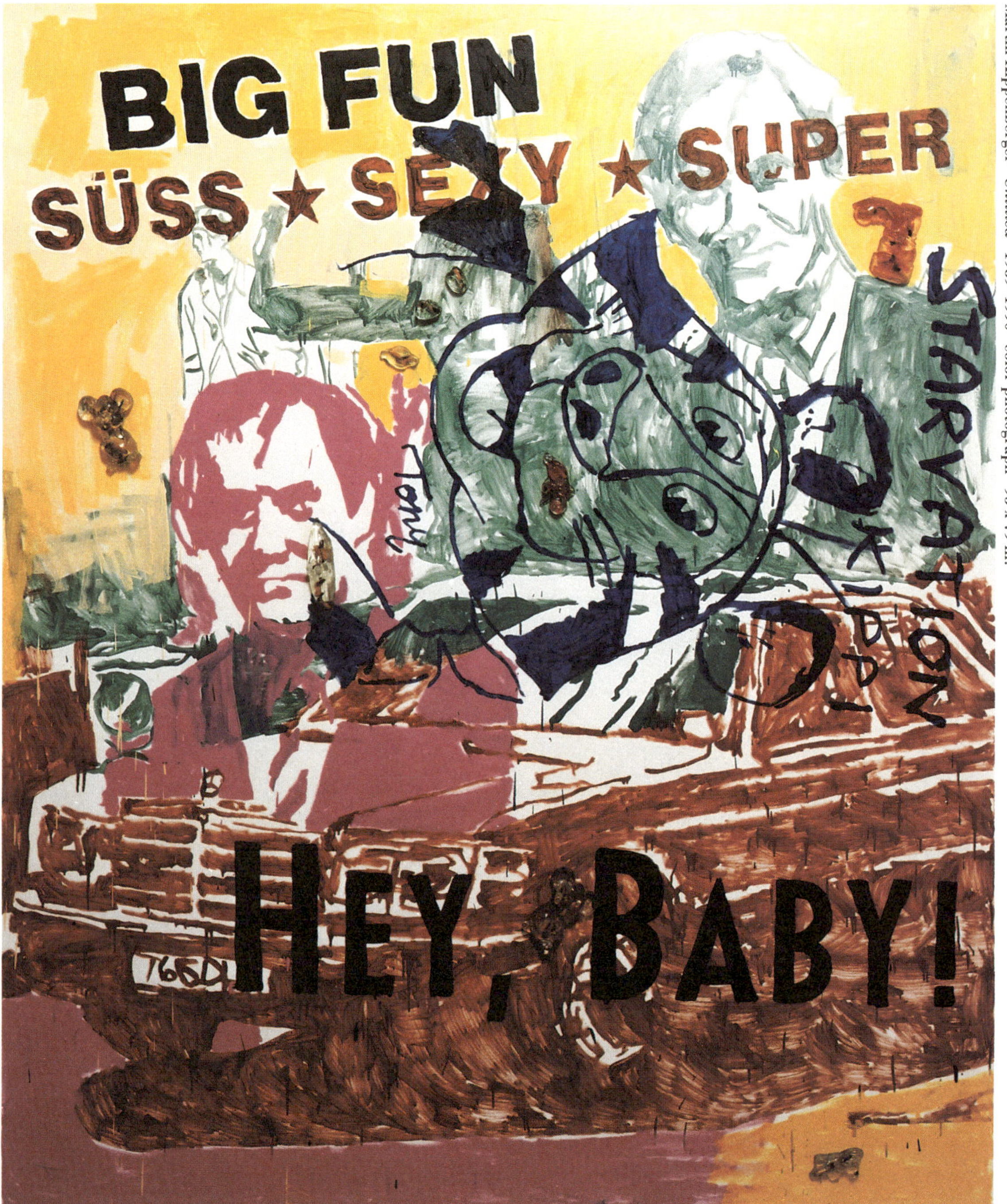

Martin Kippenberger *Untitled* 1989–1990 color photograph 95 x 79 in.

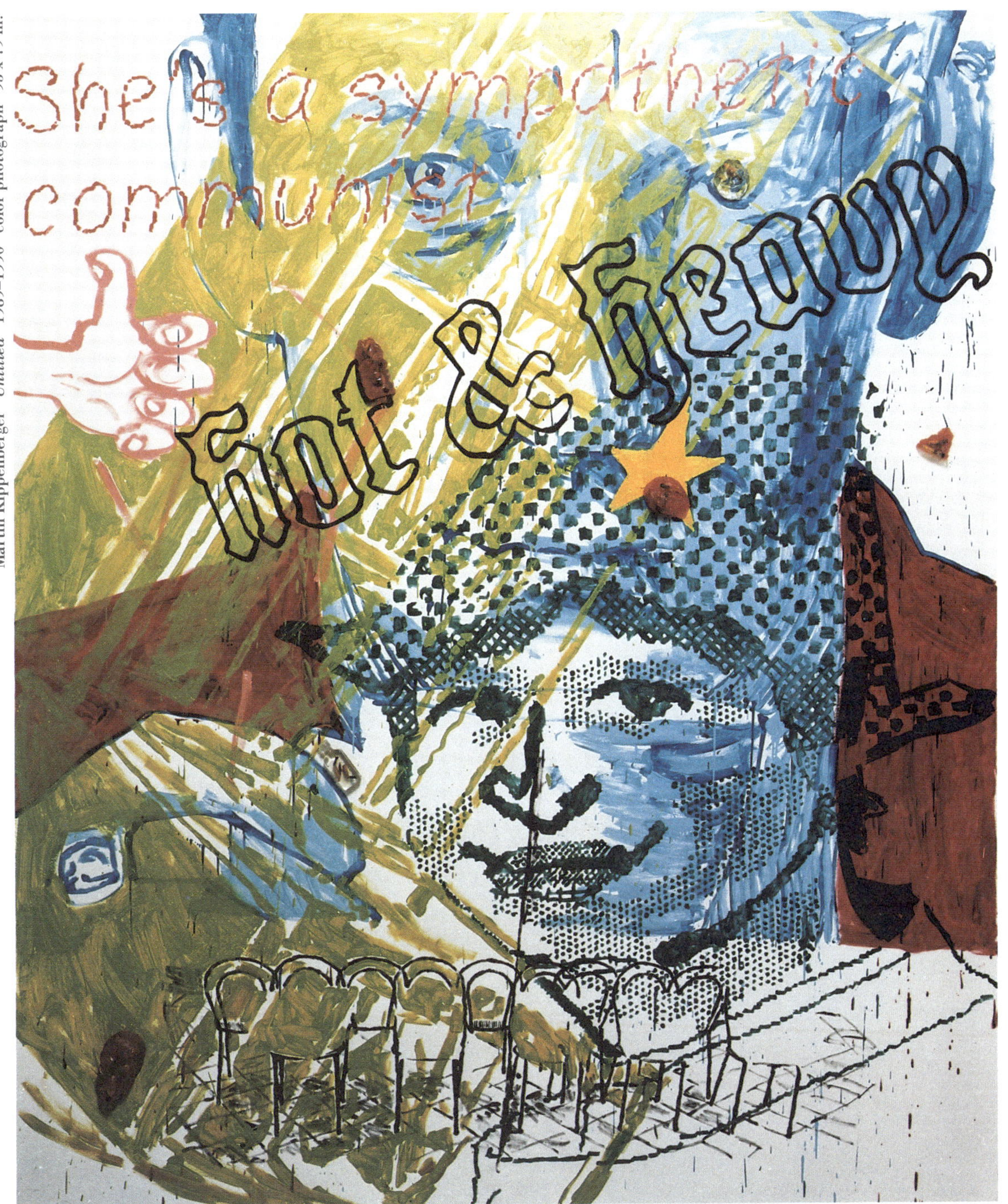

Martin Kippenberger *Untitled* 1989–1990 color photograph 95 x 79 in.

BERNHARD PRINZ

Allegorical pictures and figures have a long history in art. The work of Bernhard Prinz, a young artist living and working in Hamburg, evokes Renaissance and nineteenth-century precedents — both of which were strongly aligned with a photographlike rendering of images. Associations can also be found in his work with the social realism of the 1920s and 1930s, particularly the moralistic and allegorical figures equally dear to the authoritarian regimes of Germany and the Soviet Union. By definition, an allegory is an artistic expression in which symbolic fictional figures express truths or generalizations about human conduct or experience. It is a form to which a number of young artists in the late 1970s, often those working with the photographic medium, began to turn. Unlike many of his peers who, like the American artist Cindy Sherman, played with the potential of allegorical meanings yet avoided the literalness of allegory, Prinz has resuscitated allegory in its most traditional form.

Prinz's photographs are large, exquisitely printed, and have imposing frames that he carefully constructs. The images are often paired with sculptures, which then appear in the photographs with the figures. The photographs are simple in form and composition. Figures are centrally framed and of heroic scale. They assume poses, wear costumes, and hold props. They are seductive and alluring but aloof. What truths might they presume to reveal?

The female figures in Prinz's work often appear as personifications of virtues or as carriers of attributes of knowledge, art, sculpture, and architecture. They appear to represent higher values of learning and civilization. Male figures have been portrayed in a series as sports types; they seem to embody conditions in which aggressive actions are mediated by elaborate, agreed-upon rules and procedures, a different form of civilizing conventions. In *Zwei Eier im Glas* (*Two Eggs in Glass*) (1987), the egg may suggest fertility, while the glass may represent fragility. The suggestion of mirroring reinforces perceptions of both replication and brittleness. Three small panels with still lifes have been placed under the large central panel, duplicating the structure of a Renaissance altarpiece. As in a Renaissance painting, these still lifes are much more elaborate scenarios amplifying the grander, more simplified central panel. The images seem to embody an idea of the fragility of order and structure, suggesting the tenuous balance between creativity and destruction that civilization maintains.

Prinz seems intent on retrieving historical meanings and forms, particularly the neoclassical traditions of the last century, that have been distorted or lost; he carefully restructures and places them under the scrutinizing lens of the camera and the reflective glass of the picture. He works to heal the rupture of this tradition, inflicted by the Nazis, whose use of mythic and allegorical figures represented their perceptions of ideal, pure human types and orders of civilization. But Prinz undermines the simplistic exploitation of such figures by authoritarian regimes. By using doubles or slight permutations in a series, as in *Drei Allegorien* (*Three Allegories*) (1989), he checks our abilities to compare and contrast, to understand distinctions, and to realize the artificiality of images in which we might place truth. The subtitle of *Drei Allegorien — Idee-Ideal-Ideologie* (*Idea-Ideal-Ideology*) — suggests the process by which the immediacy of thought hardens into belief. Thus, Prinz's pictures are separate from earlier historical works in their feeling of fragility, subtlety, and transparency of construction. They avoid the traces of dogmatism and moral superiority that so often have been carried by allegorical figures. They retain an elegance, beauty, and radiance to which, he seems to suggest, civilization might aspire.

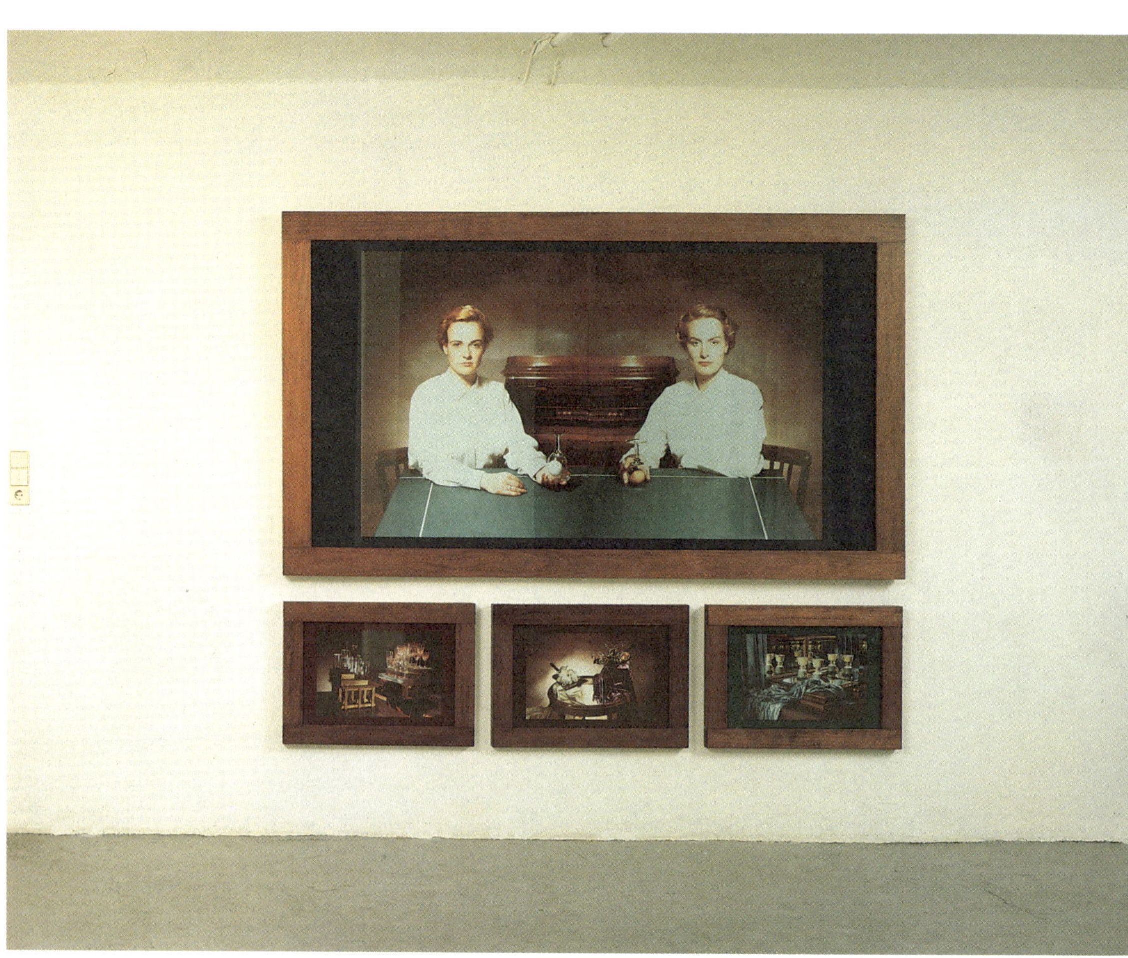

Bernhard Prinz *Zwei Eier im Glas* (*Two Eggs in Glass*) with *Scylla und Charybdis* (*Scylla and Charybdis*), *Hochzeit zu Kanaan* (*Marriage at Cana*), and *Doppeltes Lottchen* (*Double Little Lotte*) 1987 four Cibachrome photographs in wood frames 86 x 98 1/2 in. overall

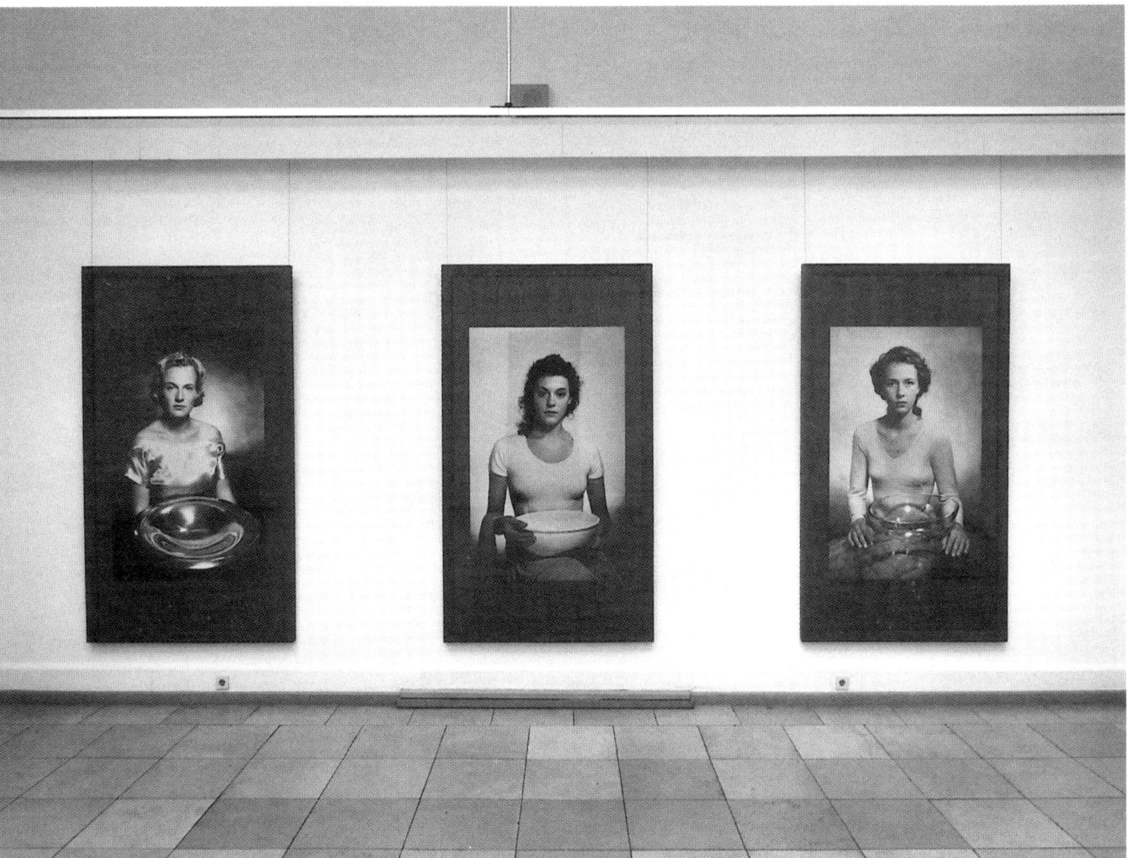

Bernhard Prinz *Drei Allegorien: Idee-Ideal-Ideologie (Three Allegories: Idea-Ideal-Ideology)* 1989 three Cibachrome photographs 94 1/2 x 52 3/4 in. each

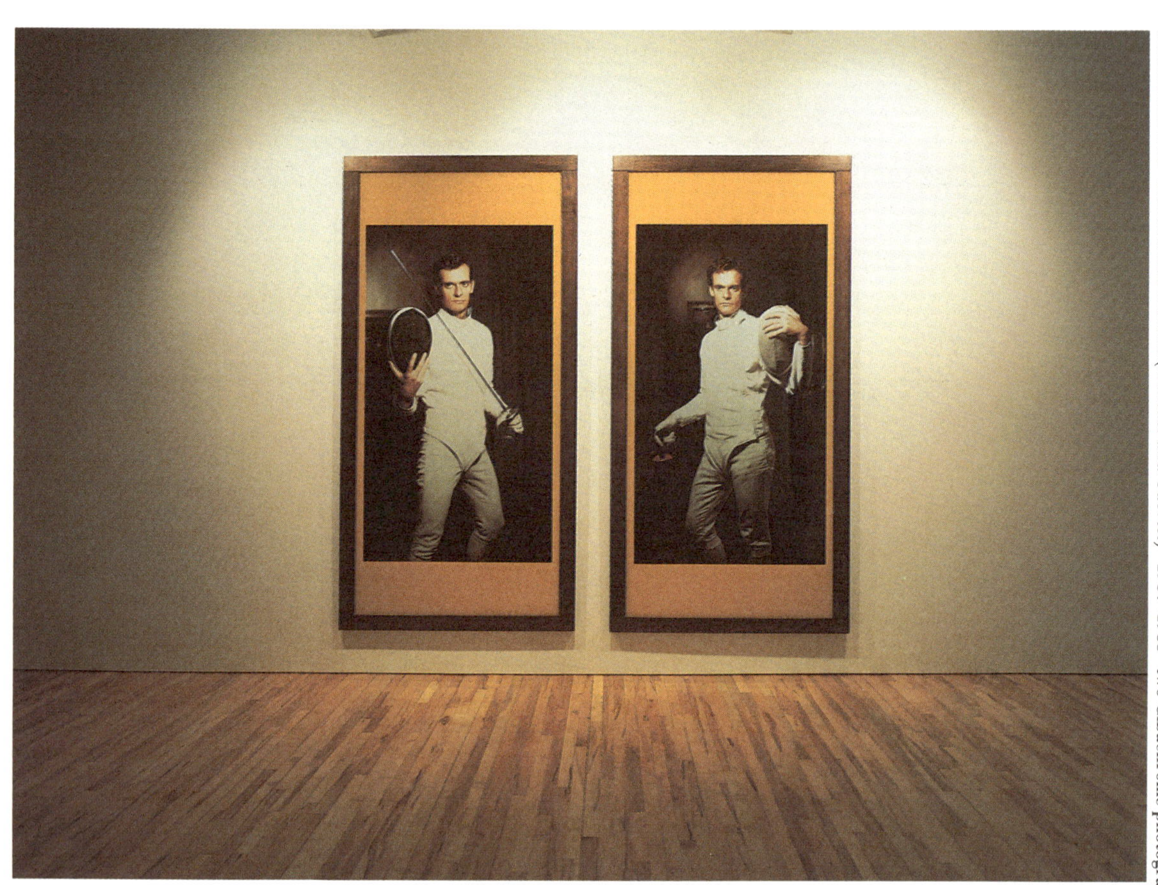

Bernhard Prinz *Michael und Gabriel (Michael and Gabriel)* 1987–1988 two Cibachrome photographs 107 1/4 x 54 in. each

GÜNTHER FÖRG

Günther Förg is an artist who devotes equal attention to a variety of media — painting, photography, sculpture, drawing, and printmaking. Concentration on and concern about surface, space, and architecture are evident in his work in all forms. Förg studied in Munich in the mid-1970s with Gerhard Merz, whose work also is involved with relationships between painting, sculpture, and architecture, and who also produced large-scale photographs. Yet Förg's strongest influence probably has been the work of Blinky Palermo, a close friend and colleague of Imi Knoebel in Düsseldorf, who died in 1976 at age thirty-four. Palermo's abstract works dealing with color, materials, and space are not so well known in the United States but are immensely important in contemporary German art.

Förg's work is highly formal and abstract, renewing issues that were central to the evolution of modernism in the 1920s and 1930s, especially in the work of Kazimir Malevich and Piet Mondrian. While Förg makes paintings like his predecessors, he also works directly on the wall, creating simple, clear fields of color. In doing so, he reduces the architectural functions of the wall; he accentuates the wall as a plane, removing it from space and transforming it into an abstract surface. In an even more radical step, Förg frequently combines wall painting with photography, superimposing very large-scale photographs, often of architectural subjects, on top of the wall painting. The photographs emphasize the illusion of the image, the feeling of the picture as a window into space. They are of a size that approximates real scale, or at least give the viewer the impression of being able to enter into a real space. The use of such scale verges on the cinematic, and the feeling created is that of encountering a frozen film. Rather than existing as brilliant Technicolor images, though, Förg's photographs are often black-and-white; so while they are contemporary, they appear historically removed. In some photographs the colors are naturalistic, muted, and tonal. They appear as soft and dreamlike. Sometimes the photographer's spectral, transparent image is caught in the photograph as a reflection, adding to the unreality of the image and to the ambiguity of time.

The subjects of Förg's photographs often have been icons of modernist architecture, such as the Barcelona Pavilion of Mies van der Rohe, the Gropius buildings of the Bauhaus in Dessau, and the Villa of Ludwig Wittgenstein in Vienna. The photographs portray these structures as rationalized and abstract yet romantic intersections of planes and light. Windows and doors penetrate the solid planes of the walls with which they are contrasted by being both transparent and reflective. The wall paintings on which these photographs are often presented assume even more the state of being neither architectural nor pictorial; they are perhaps as close as it is possible to come to a modernist ideal of non-illusion in art.

Förg attempts to recapture and resuscitate the romantic utopianism of modernism, before the modernist impulse was forever shattered by World War II. Even as he understands and extends the possibilities of high modernism, a sense of nostalgia and loss pervades the work. The photographs interrupt the seamlessness of the plane. They are like a looking glass into which one could fall backward — into a time before the tragedy of the war struck. Occasionally, Förg introduces a photograph with a human figure into an installation. When the human form enters this world, it seems to be only a visitor, evoking desire and vulnerability. In general, Förg's work recalls a Platonistic view of the world — that the world we see is one of illusions and that the real world, ordered by perfection, is one of abstract geometries. The colored wall painting is resolutely of the world; the photograph becomes a false window into history.

Günther Förg Installation view, Wiener Sezession, Vienna 1990

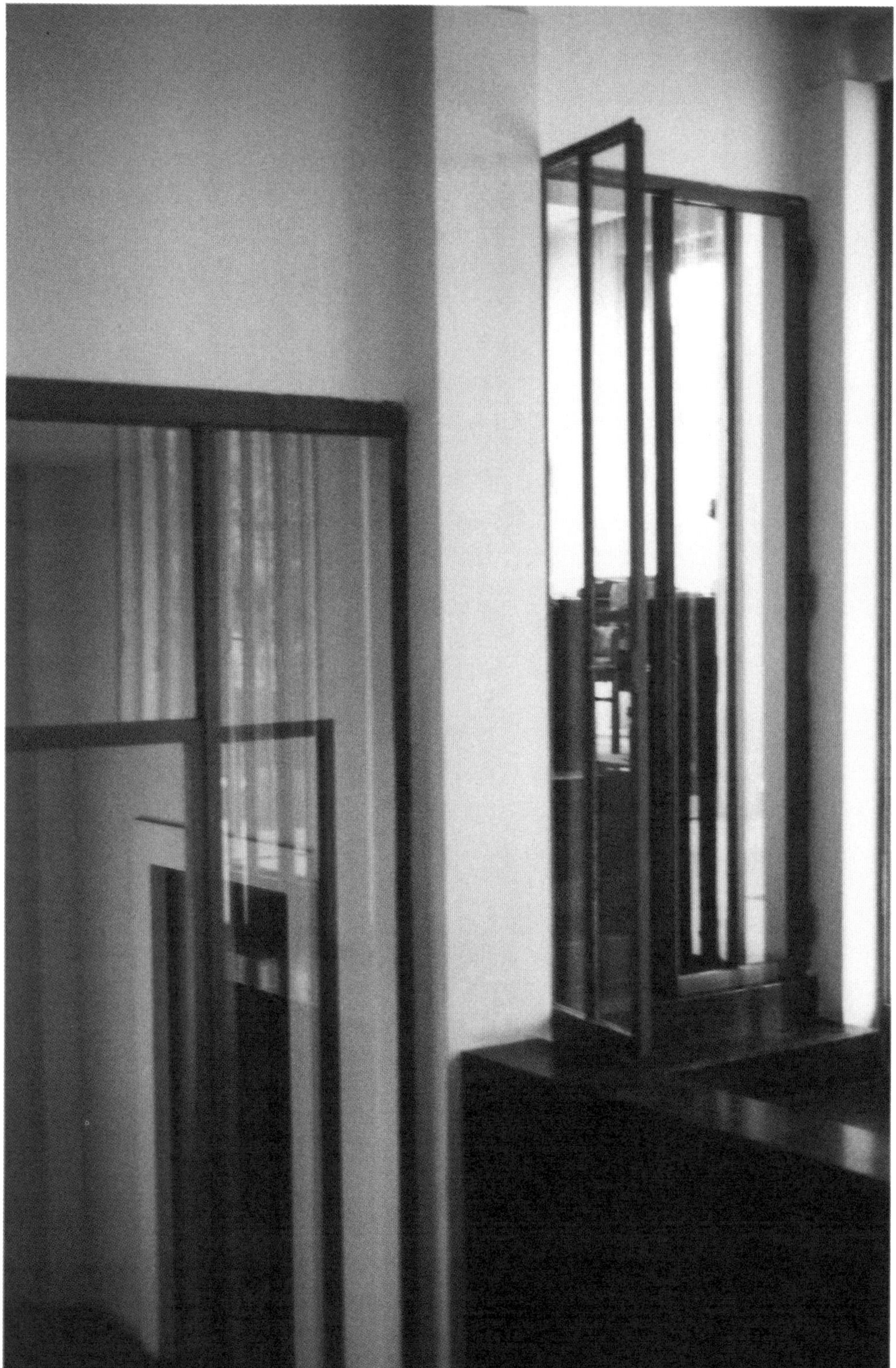

Günther Förg *Villa Wittgenstein 26/87* 1986–1987 color photograph 100 1/2 x 51 1/4 in.

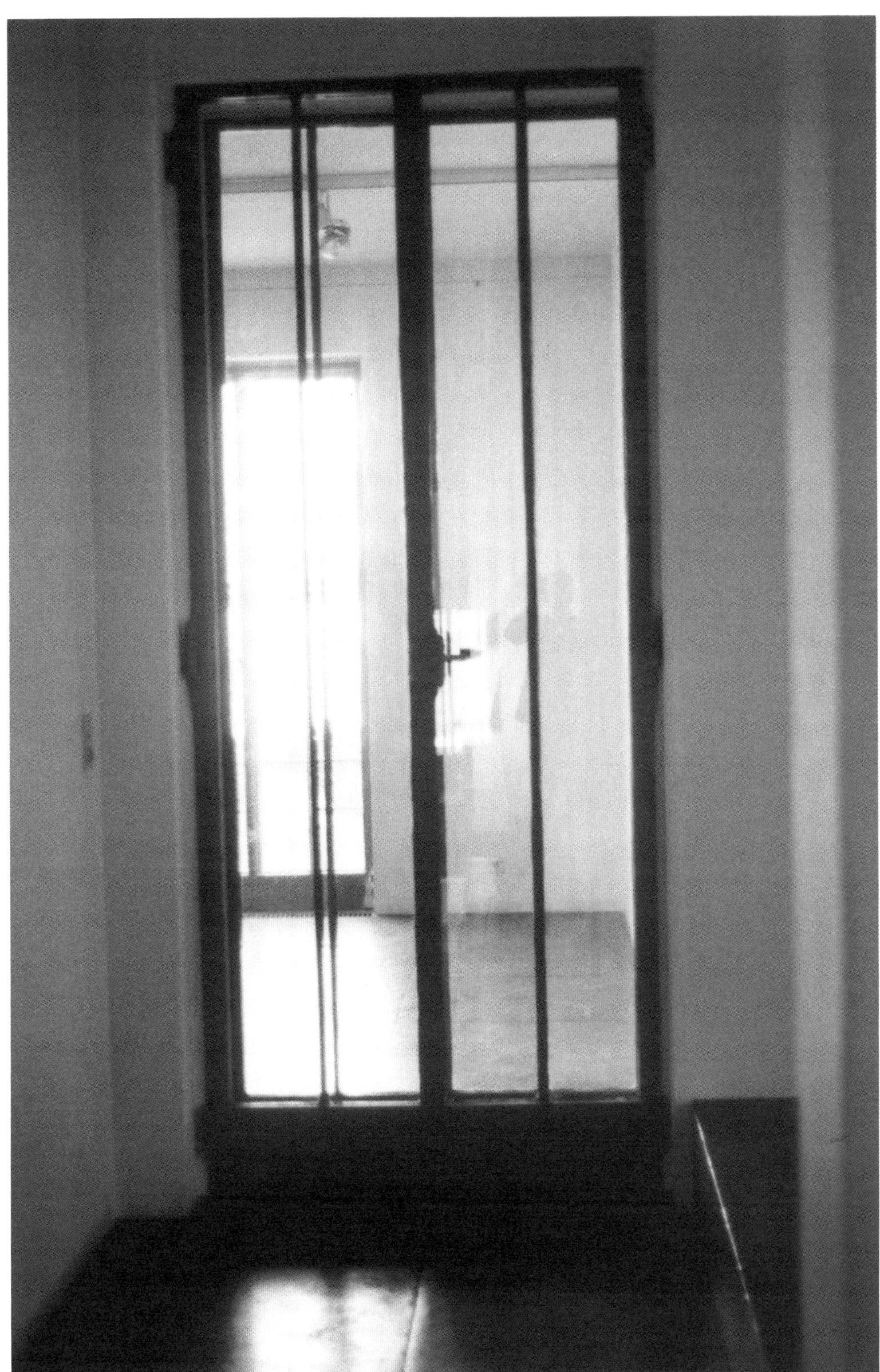

Günther Förg *Villa Wittgenstein 27/87* 1986–1987 color photograph 100 1/2 x 51 1/4 in.

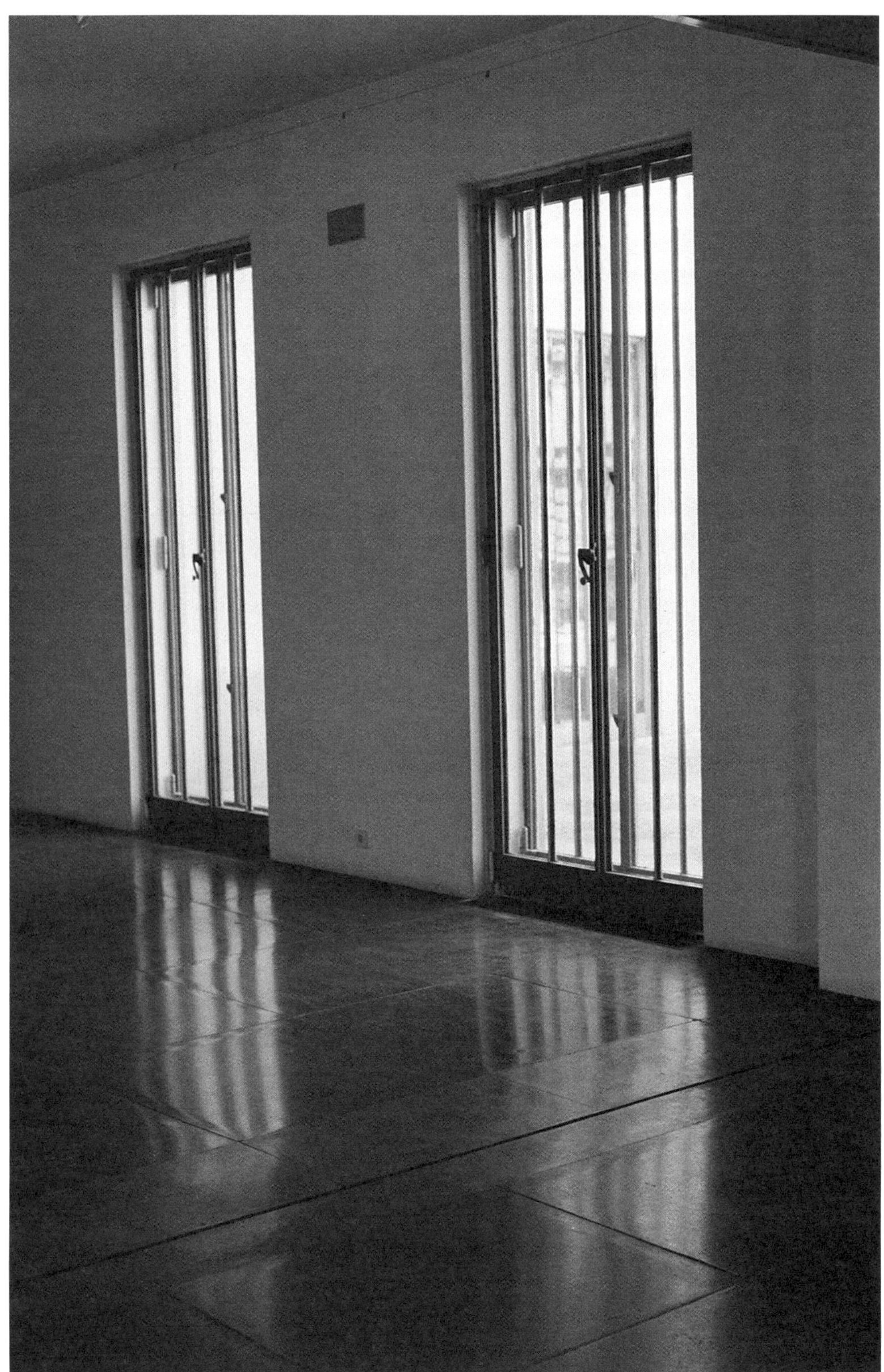

Günther Förg *Villa Wittgenstein 28/87* 1986–1987 color photograph 100 1/2 x 51 1/4 in.

REINHARD MUCHA

Although Reinhard Mucha is usually referred to as a sculptor, photographs are frequently at the heart of his work. Architecture, too, is vital for him as the frame in which his objects reside and as a space shared between objects and audience. In this way, his work reveals debts to Minimalism in its physical presence but also in its cool and obsessive control of materials. Unlike Minimalist works, however, each of his pieces is carefully handcrafted. Mucha, like many young artists who live and work in Düsseldorf, continues to extend the influence of Joseph Beuys. This is evident in Mucha's presentation of objects as tableaux and in vitrines. Like Beuys, too, he uses nonart materials or objects in an attempt to bridge the gap between life and art.

The early work shown in this exhibition, *Untitled* (1980), consists of five museum display cases, each paired with a simple chair. In the center of each case Mucha has placed a small black-and-white photograph, framed and standing. Within the case to one side near the photograph is a closed, polished, gray painted-wood box. On the other side is a polished, gray painted-wood structure, similar to the box. It is as if the box has been enlarged and opened, positioned over the glass of the case, covering and partially hiding its interior. Everything about the five vitrines is nearly identical, except for the image in the photographs. Each photograph has an elderberry bush in full bloom as its subject. The bush sits in full view at the center, like the subject of a conventional, family-portrait snapshot. Protected and preserved within the case, this image becomes enormously precious. It seems to stand in for something or even someone who is absent. Mucha has captured a fundamental quality of photographs: the representation of something that is not present, something that acts as an index of things outside, of things in life beyond the frame.

By using museum display cases, which traditionally hold objects of historical value, Mucha reinforces the idea that the photograph has an archival function; it holds a memory, acting as a key to history. But here the image seems mundane and personal; it is secret in its meaning to all except the photographer. Mucha has entitled each elderberry photograph with the name of a small German town. His choice of the elderberry is particular, as the bush is common along the railroad lines of Germany but is generally unseen until it blooms. These railways function like the highways across the United States, linking small towns to each other and to the larger world outside. The display cases themselves are linked by prominently visible electrical cords; again, not unlike the power lines that run parallel to railroad tracks and highways.

Mucha creates works of overlaid metaphors. The photograph is framed behind a sheet of glass, visible only through the glass of the display case. The closed box is reflective, but its contents, if any, remain hidden. The open structure, mimicking the box, only partially conceals the interior view, and its felt lining absorbs the light. The felt is the only softening element among the hard surfaces of glass, steel, and painted wood. It suggests both openness and vulnerability, but it remains protected, inaccessible. The photograph held within these hard and hermetic structures seems all the more poignant and personal. It is not unlike the portrait one might see sitting on the corner of an office desk, the reminder of the personal life outside the strictures and abstract functions of work. The elderberry bush is untrimmed, wild, free in the landscape, open to the sun and air, and flourishes alongside railroad lines. Its industrial neighbor is both close and unreachable. As a photographic image, the bush has been removed from life. Like the other materials in this work, it is colorless, consisting of gradations of blacks, whites, and grays.

Despite their strong physical presence, Mucha's works are highly pictorial, layering images through transparency and reflection. The photograph, similarly, is an image frozen from patterns of light and shadow on film and paper. Mucha carefully controls how his works are photographed and reproduced, aware that the image quickly becomes a common substitute for the reality of the experience of the work itself. Often he incorporates photographs of his own works into sculptural objects he will make years later. The photograph thus becomes the bridge between experience and memory, between life and history.

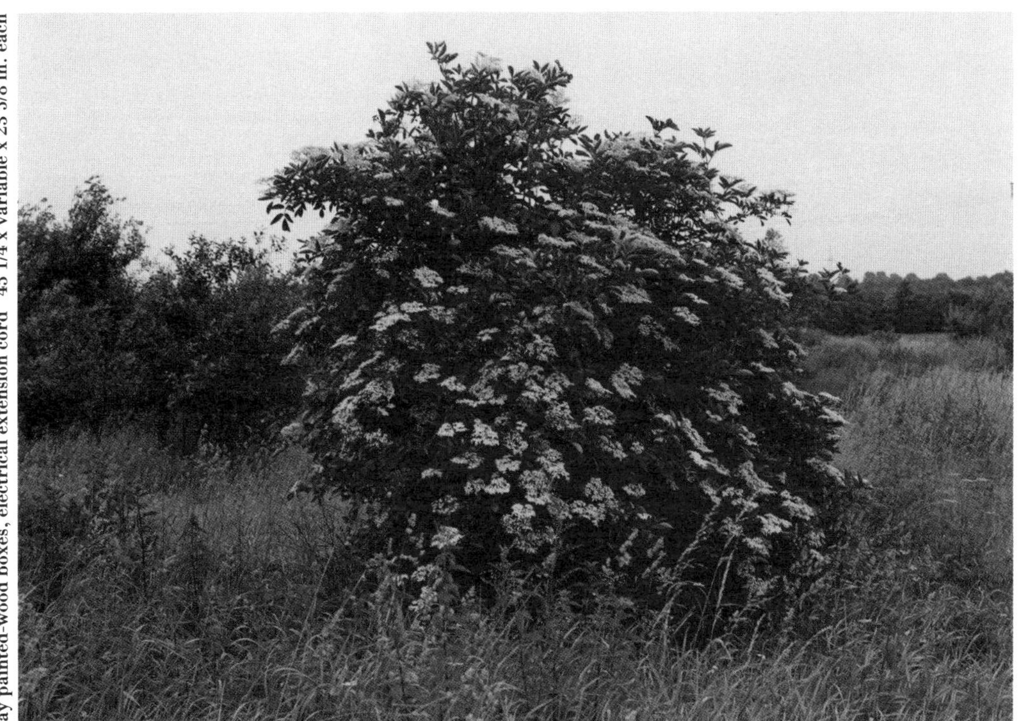

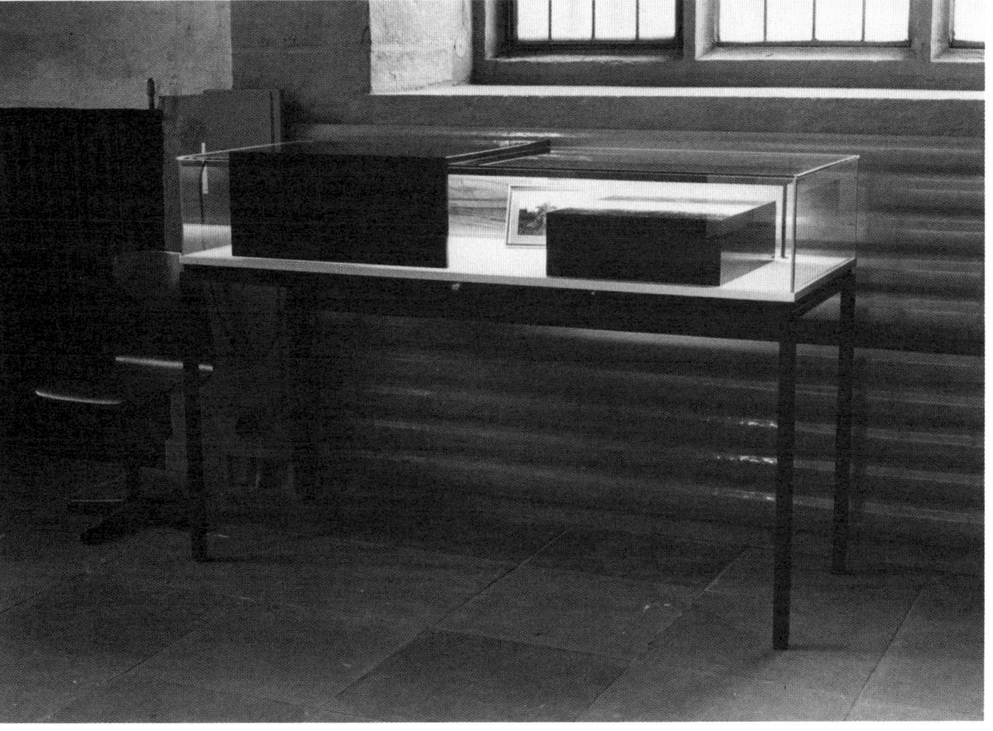

Reinhard Mucha *Untitled* 1980 five elements consisting of: chairs, illuminated exhibition vitrines, gray painted-wood coverings with felt lining, framed black-and-white photographs, gray painted-wood boxes, electrical extension cord 45 1/4 x variable x 23 5/8 in. each

APRATH

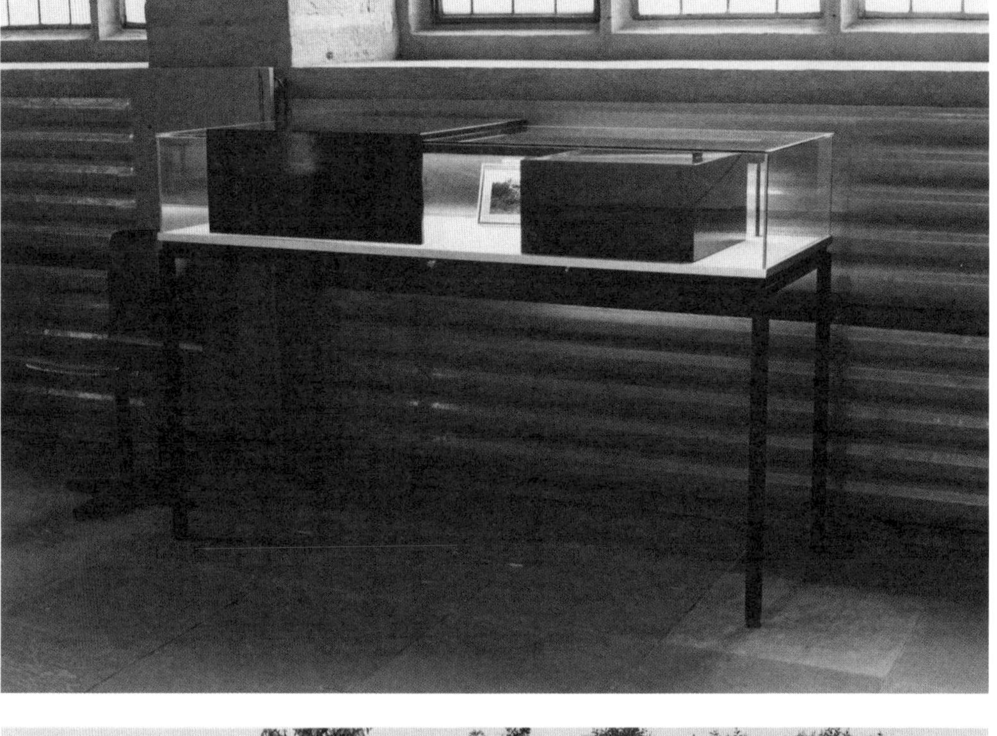

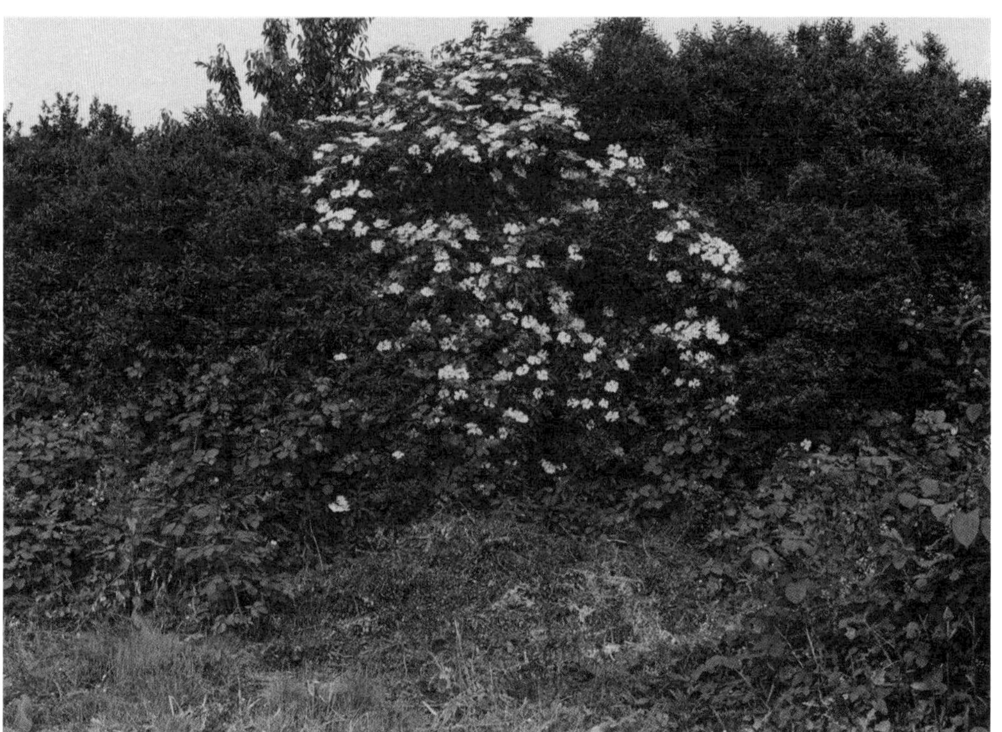

GLOGAU

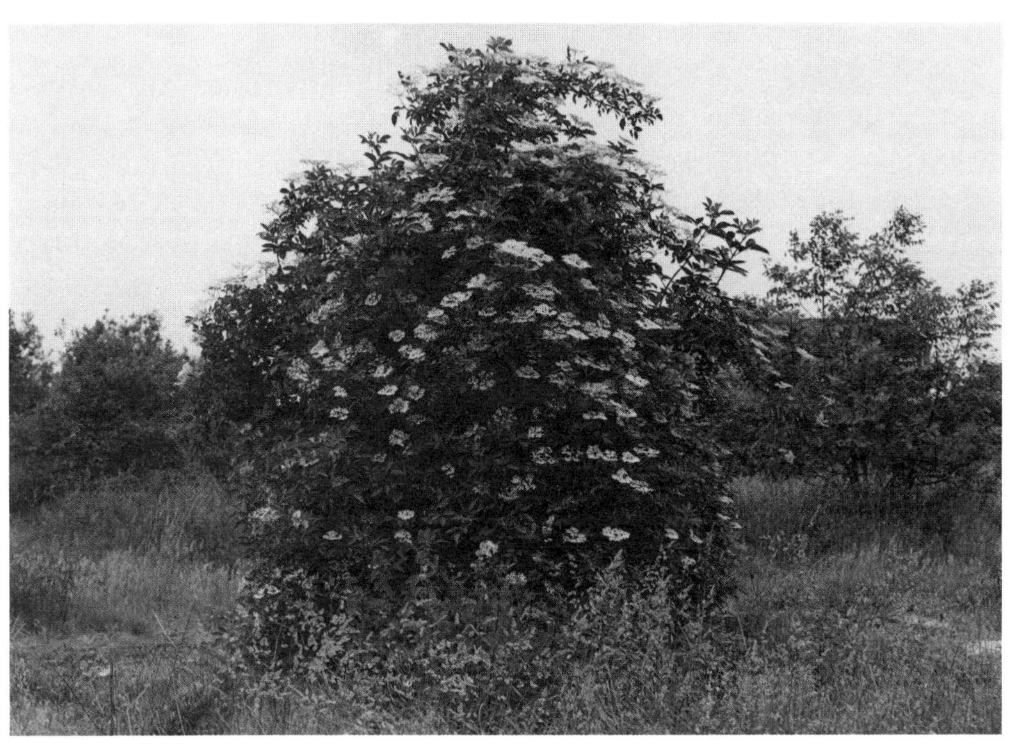

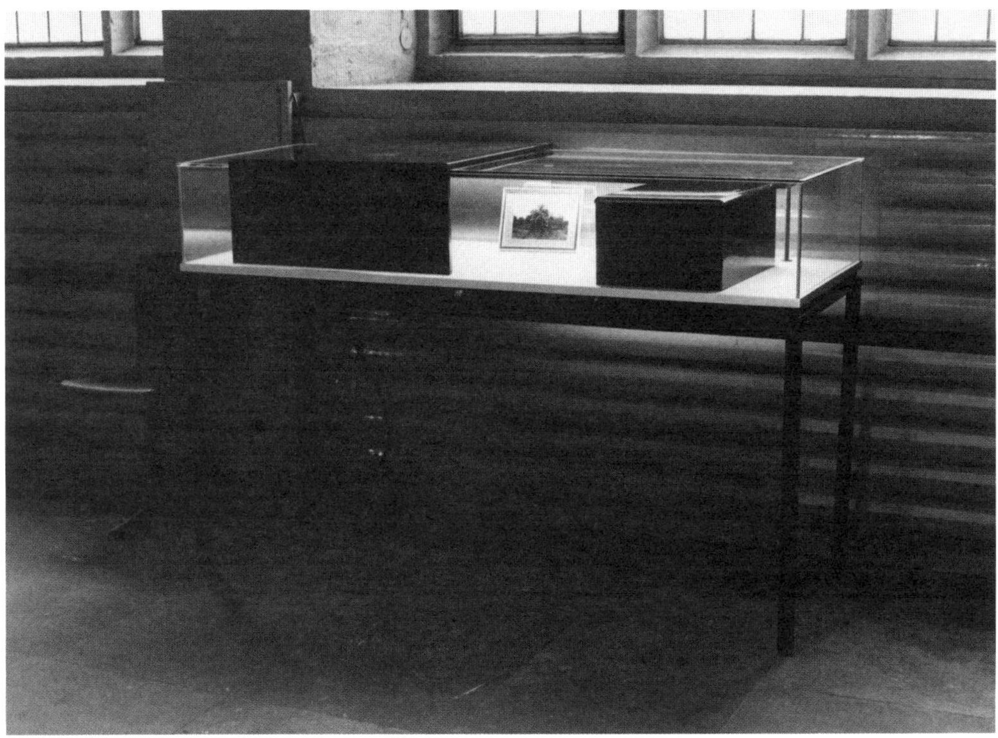

WITTEN

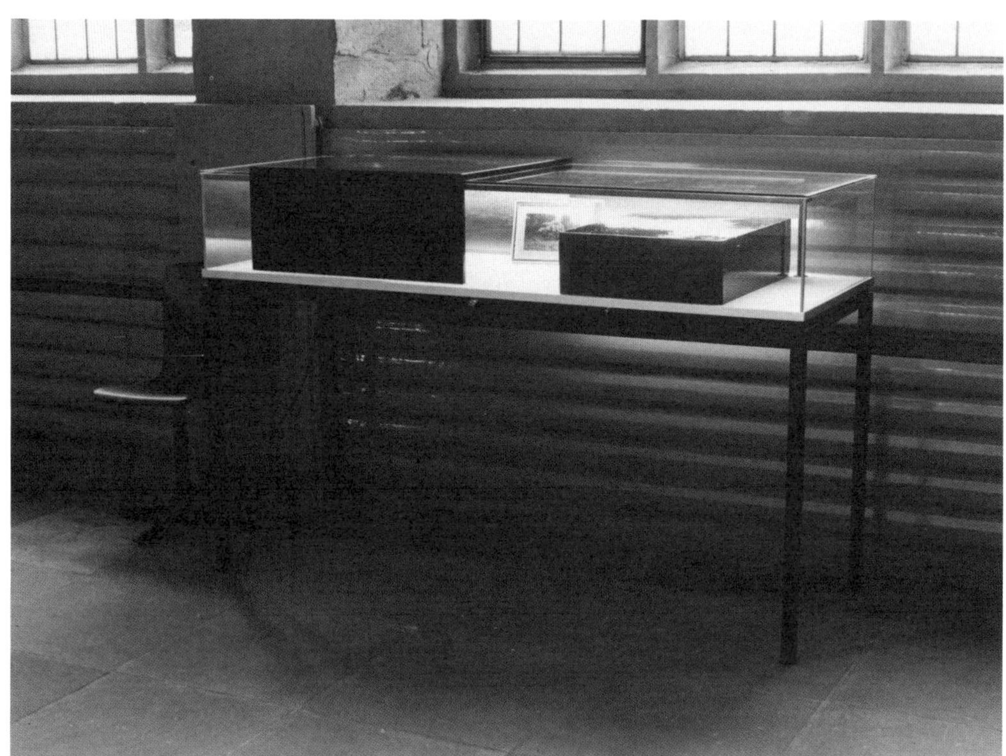

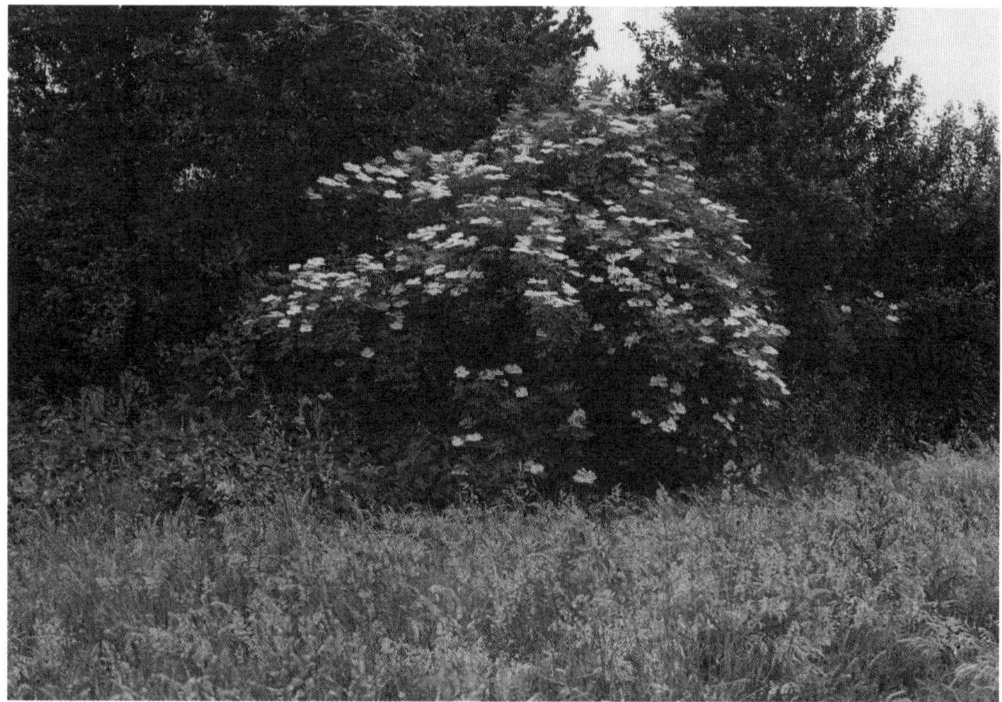

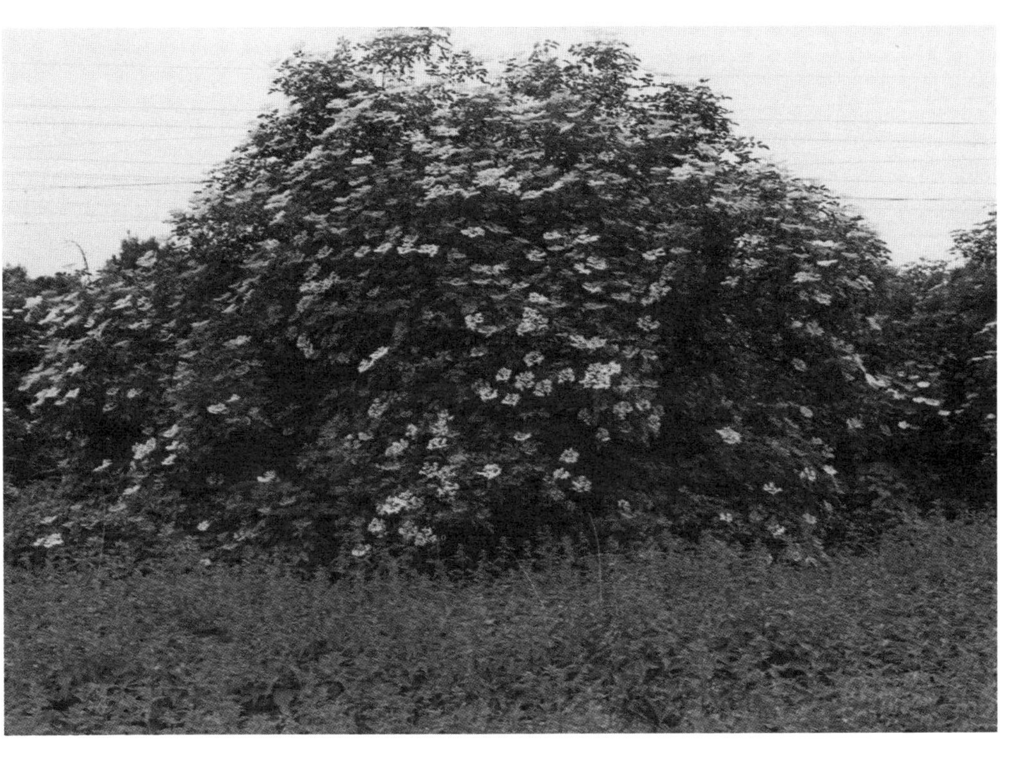

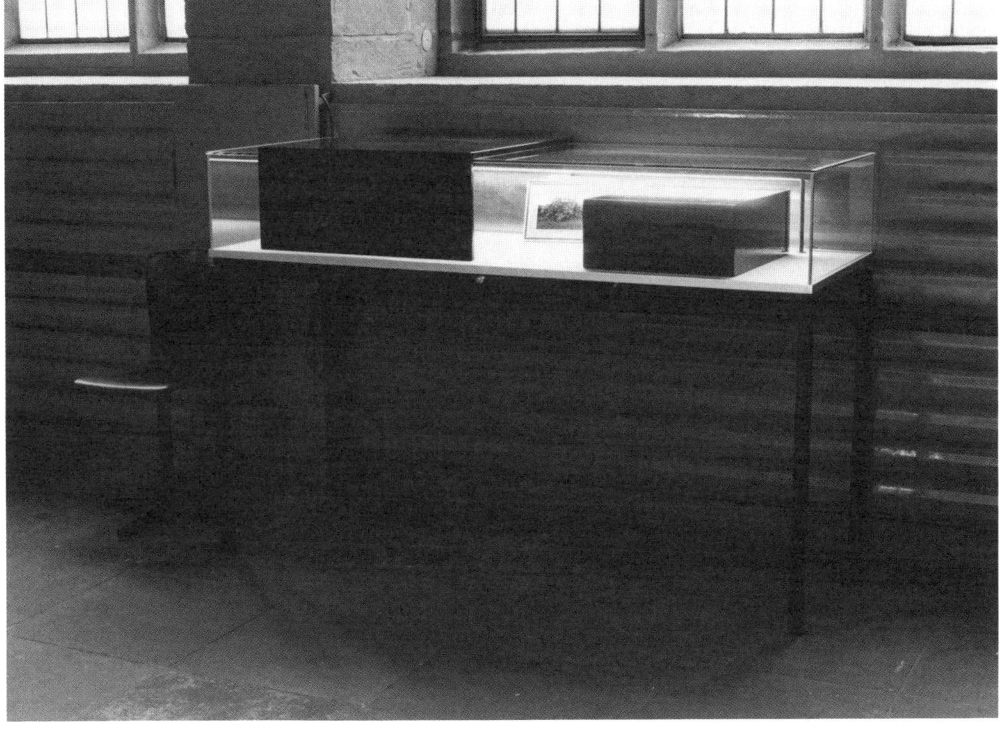

LORSCH

THOMAS STRUTH

Thomas Struth is an artist who makes pictures about social relationships. He works in series, continuing to expand upon one subject even as he takes on a separate theme, so that one series reflects on another. The works for which he first became known, made in the late 1970s and early 1980s, are views of cities, unpeopled landscapes of streets and buildings seen in carefully printed, small-scale, black-and-white photographs. As a student of Gerhard Richter, Struth approached the making of the photographic image as a relation of highly conventionalized yet subjective facts. The influence of his subsequent teachers, Bernd and Hilla Becher, is evident in his choice of subject matter as well as in many of the formal decisions he makes about how the photographs will look. Like the Bechers' photographs, too, his images of cities reveal something about the nature of the social forces that created and govern them and out of which they were constructed. Struth traveled throughout the decade, taking photographs of cities across Europe, the United States, and Japan — countries that share the social organization of late twentieth-century capitalism. The photographs show, however, each culture's specific attitude toward texture and materials, toward space and efficiency, toward public life and history.

Struth's work became more fully his own when he began exhibiting color and black-and-white photographs of families: these were single views, posed portraits, in which each family chose their own setting and grouping. Begun in 1986 but mostly made from 1988 to 1990, the portraits share much with the earlier architectural photographs. They, too, were taken on his travels in the urban, bourgeois, industrialized world. Shared ways of life are evident between various cultures and age groups, although cultural and social distinctions are also discernible. Particular relationships within the given family are also revealed, with both underlying ties and tensions frozen on the surface. Although Struth would invite a family to pose only after he had known them for a substantial period, the people in the portraits always appear self-conscious; they are aware of the making of an image. They see that the photographer is watching them, and they understand that the resulting images will become objects that the public will scrutinize relentlessly. We, the audience, in turn become voyeurs, creating stories and worlds around their exposed images.

A series of works Struth began in 1989 consists of large color photographs of galleries in museums. The subject of the photograph — a museum interior with visitors looking at or passing by historical works of art — makes us, the audience, assume multiple roles. We share with the museum visitors a relationship with the historical paintings in the photograph; we now, too, become part of that public. We also share the view of the photographer, looking at this public. The final turn comes as we realize that we ourselves are in a museum, looking at a work of art. Our experience is no longer only that of the voyeur; we are participants in the scene, not so different from the people in the photograph.

Struth, like Reinhard Mucha, is acutely aware of the role of the museum as an agent of interpretation and preservation of the work of art. Conventions for the display of and habitual ways of viewing works of art are taken for granted and become unacknowledged frames that control our experience. Struth's images begin to reveal these conventions, to allow us to see ourselves and to understand our experiences with critical self-awareness. He explores the degrees of understanding that we can gain by looking at images, realizing that all images are constructed, and that they share and reveal the social forms by which we structure our lives. The process of looking becomes at once a trigger to the mind and a stopping point, a means of reflection.

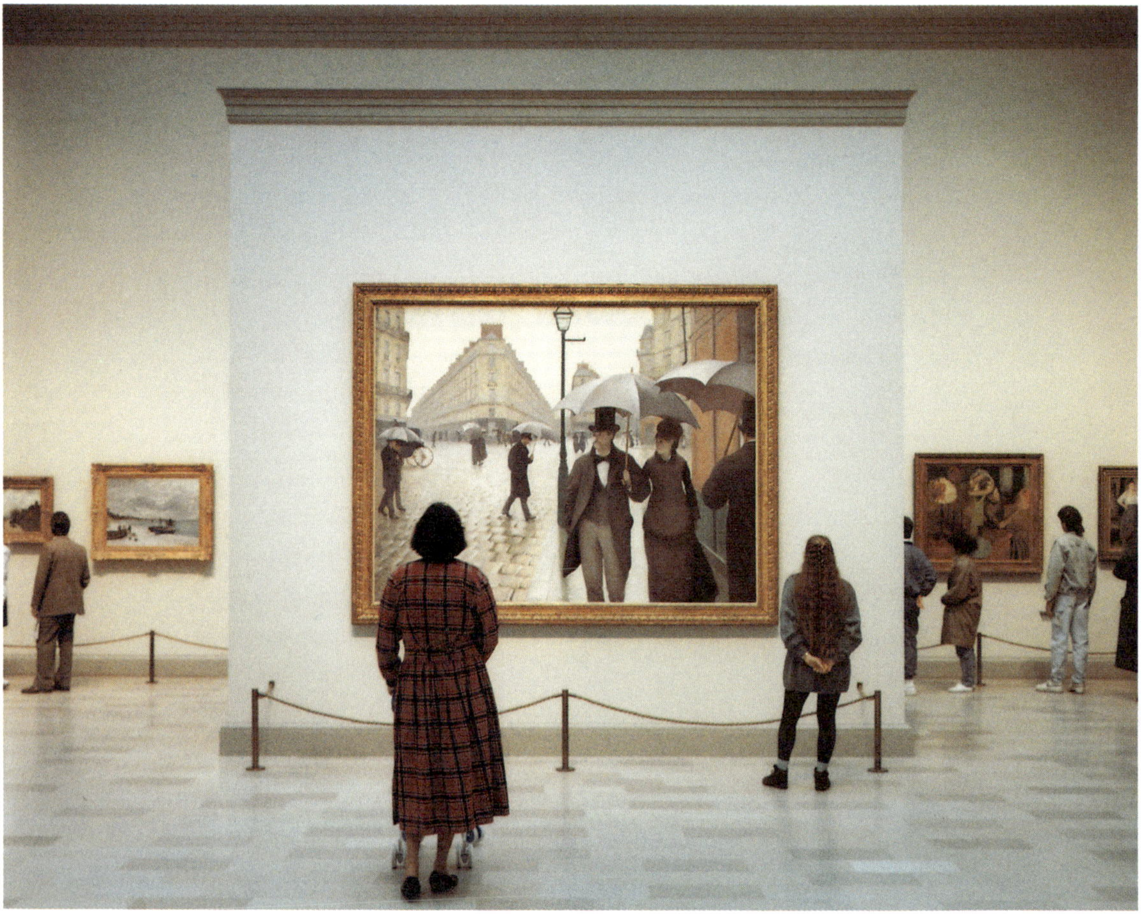

Thomas Struth *Art Institute of Chicago I* 1990 color photograph mounted on Plexiglas 68 1/2 x 81 in.

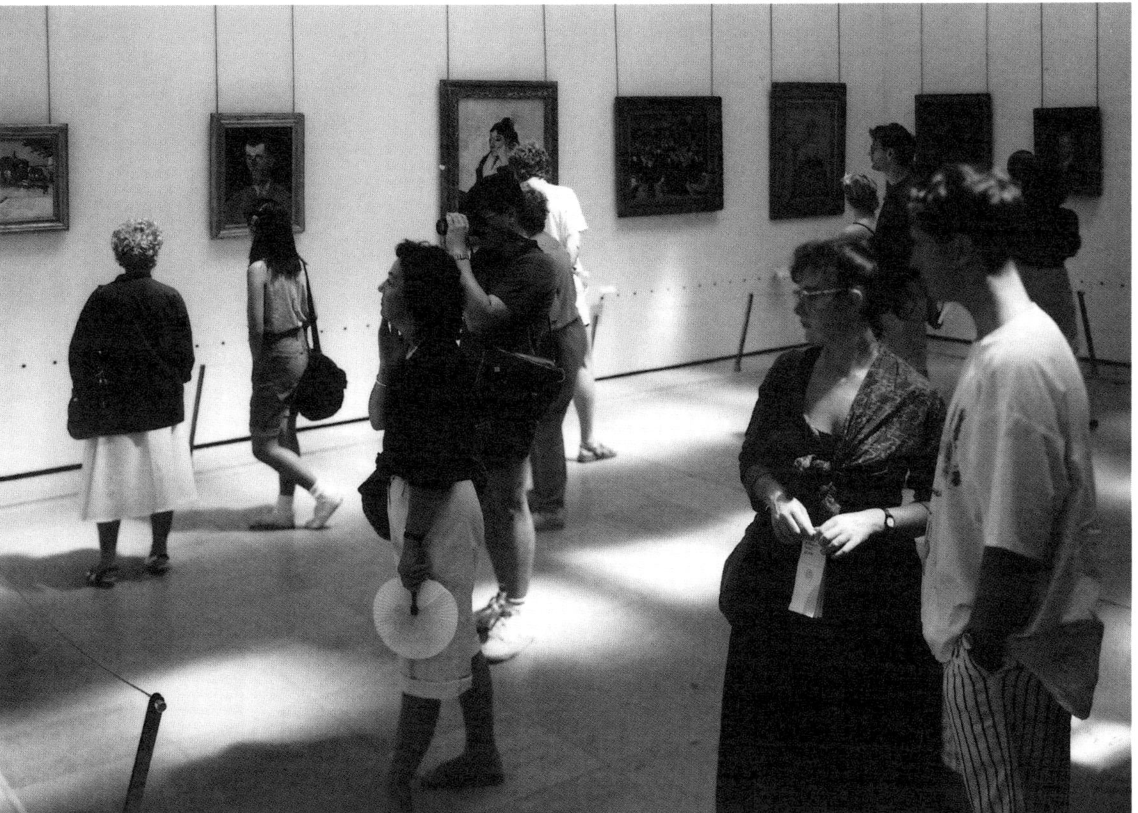

Thomas Struth *Musée d'Orsay I* 1989 color photograph mounted on Plexiglas 57 7/8 x 71 5/8 in.

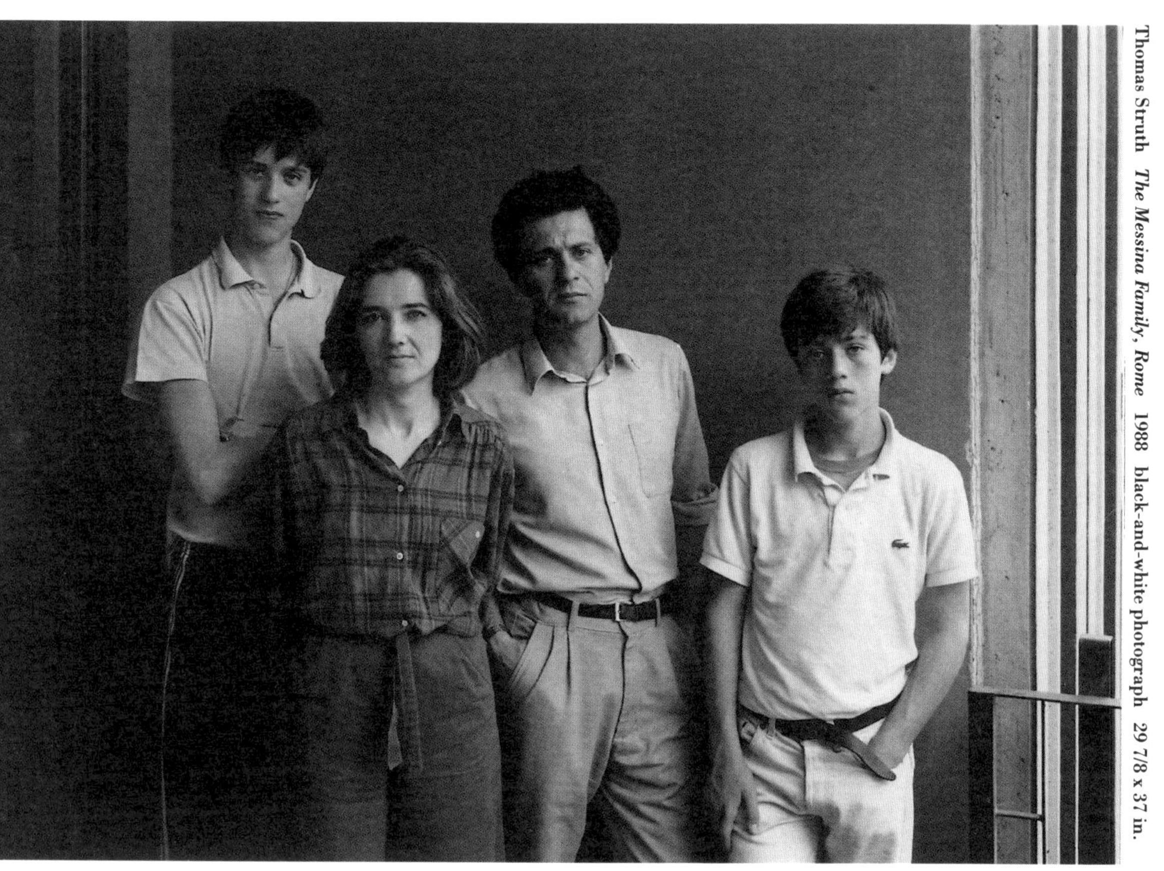

Thomas Struth *The Messina Family, Rome* 1988 black-and-white photograph 29 7/8 x 37 in.

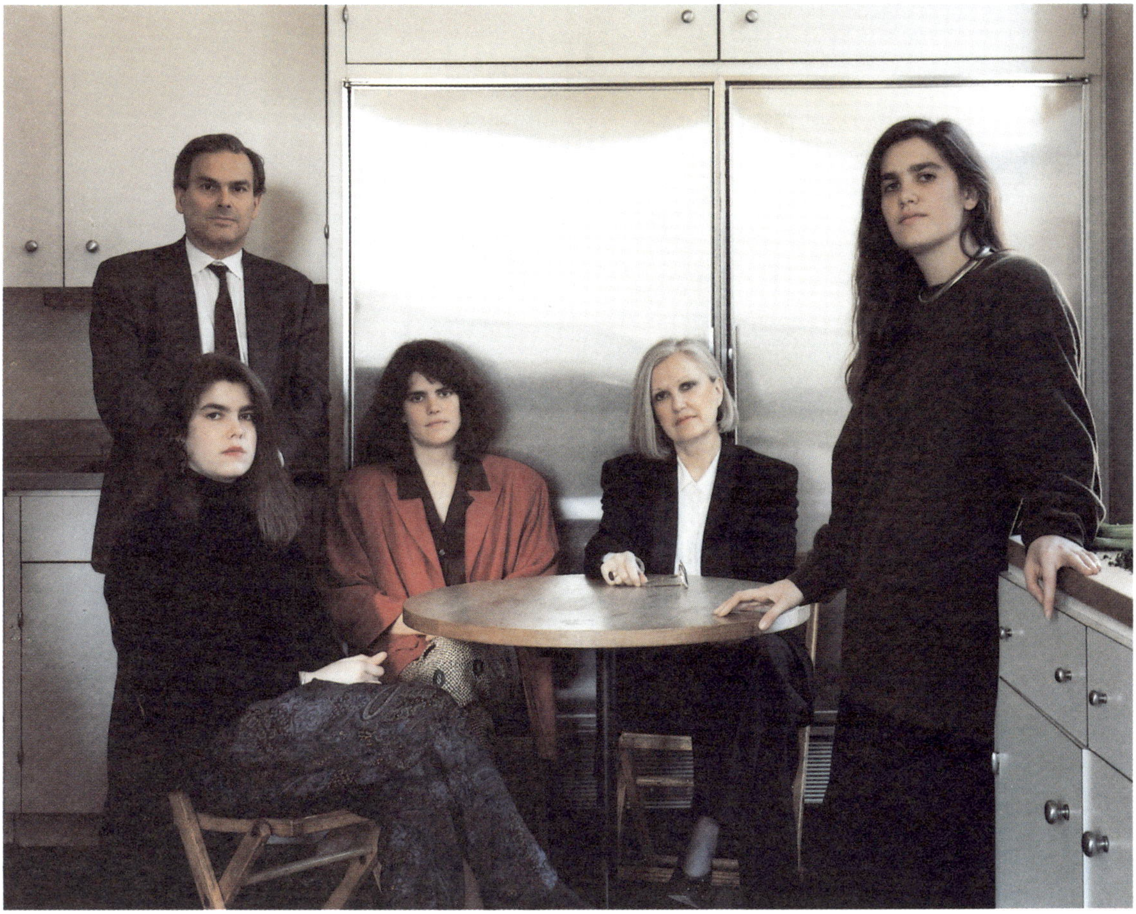

Thomas Struth *The Ghez Family, Chicago* 1990 color photograph 40 1/8 x 46 3/4 in.

THOMAS RUFF

Thomas Ruff began making portrait photographs in 1981, taking as his subject the young people around him in the milieu of the Düsseldorf art academy. A student of Bernd Becher, his work shows the Bechers' influence through its consistent framing and vantage point, neutral background, even lighting, work on one subject type in a series, and choice of a common but overlooked subject. Ruff also builds on the precedent of the German photographer August Sander, who made an extensive series of portraits in the 1920s and 1930s, not of individuals as such but as representative types of various social backgrounds and occupations.

While Ruff has drawn on the strengths of the Bechers' work, his photographs reflect the style and concerns of his own generation. His portraits are highly contemporary, while at the same time preserving and contributing to history a vision of a specific moment and generation. Like many other younger artists using photography, he frequently makes photographs in which beautiful color and large scale are integral to the overall effect. They are commanding in their presence and alluring in their beauty — stylish and self-assured. The similar structure of the portraits and their linkage as a series emphasize not the individuality or personality of the subjects but their relationship as types. While Ruff's subjects are from Düsseldorf, their expressions and attitudes, clothes and hairstyles, are typical of middle-class young people from almost anywhere in the urban, industrialized West. Their images retain the commonality of an international youth culture, poised to take up prescribed positions within their respective societies.

In 1986 Ruff shifted the scale of the portraits, giving them an outsize, larger-than-life cinematic grandeur. The subjects of the portraits took on the character of ingenuous stars. One cannot help but recall Andy Warhol's dictum that in a world dominated by mass media everyone would be famous for fifteen minutes. But unlike the figures who became stars of the Warholian underground, Ruff's young people maintain an unselfconscious innocence, an ordinariness of style and bearing, suggesting the image of an uncalculated persona. To date he has produced more than one hundred such portraits.

While making the portraits, Ruff also collected newspaper photographs, periodically and unsystematically clipped from one of the larger German newspapers, the name of which he refuses to reveal in order to avoid specific associations. He began rephotographing these black-and-white reproductions, saved over a period of ten years, in tonal color. He then printed them at twice their original scale, reinforcing the graininess and distortion of the images. Not unlike the portraits, the newspaper photographs reveal Ruff's fascination with a salvation of the commonplace, or, as he has said, with "giving worth to ordinary subjects."[1] This work represents a renewal and permutation of the earlier works of Gerhard Richter and Hans-Peter Feldmann, also based on newspaper photographs. However, typical of the current generation, Ruff places high value on craft, careful production, and elegance of presentation. A self-consciousness and an appreciation of style separate this work from its precedents and unite the newspaper photographs with his earlier portraits.

Although at first the two bodies of Ruff's work seen here — portraits and newspaper photographs — appear to be disparate, they are logical and consistent in their common concerns. The particularities of personality and the narratives of story, or, in short, the potential for information available from the photograph, have been neutralized. Instead, the photograph is seen as an object in itself, a surface onto which meanings are projected, our own fascinations fetishized.

1 Conversation with the artist, June 12, 1991.

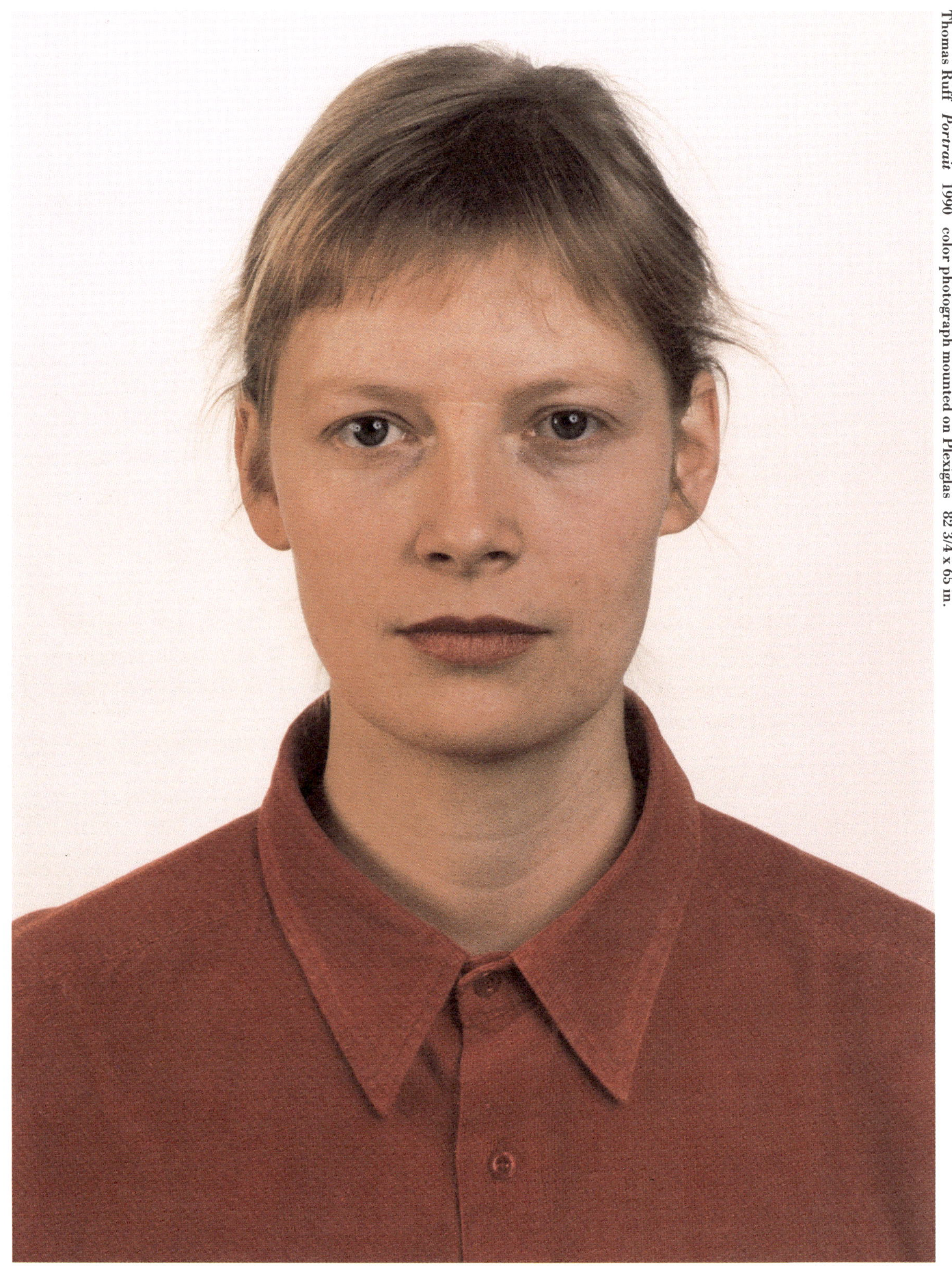

Thomas Ruff *Portrait* 1990 color photograph mounted on Plexiglas 82 3/4 x 65 in.

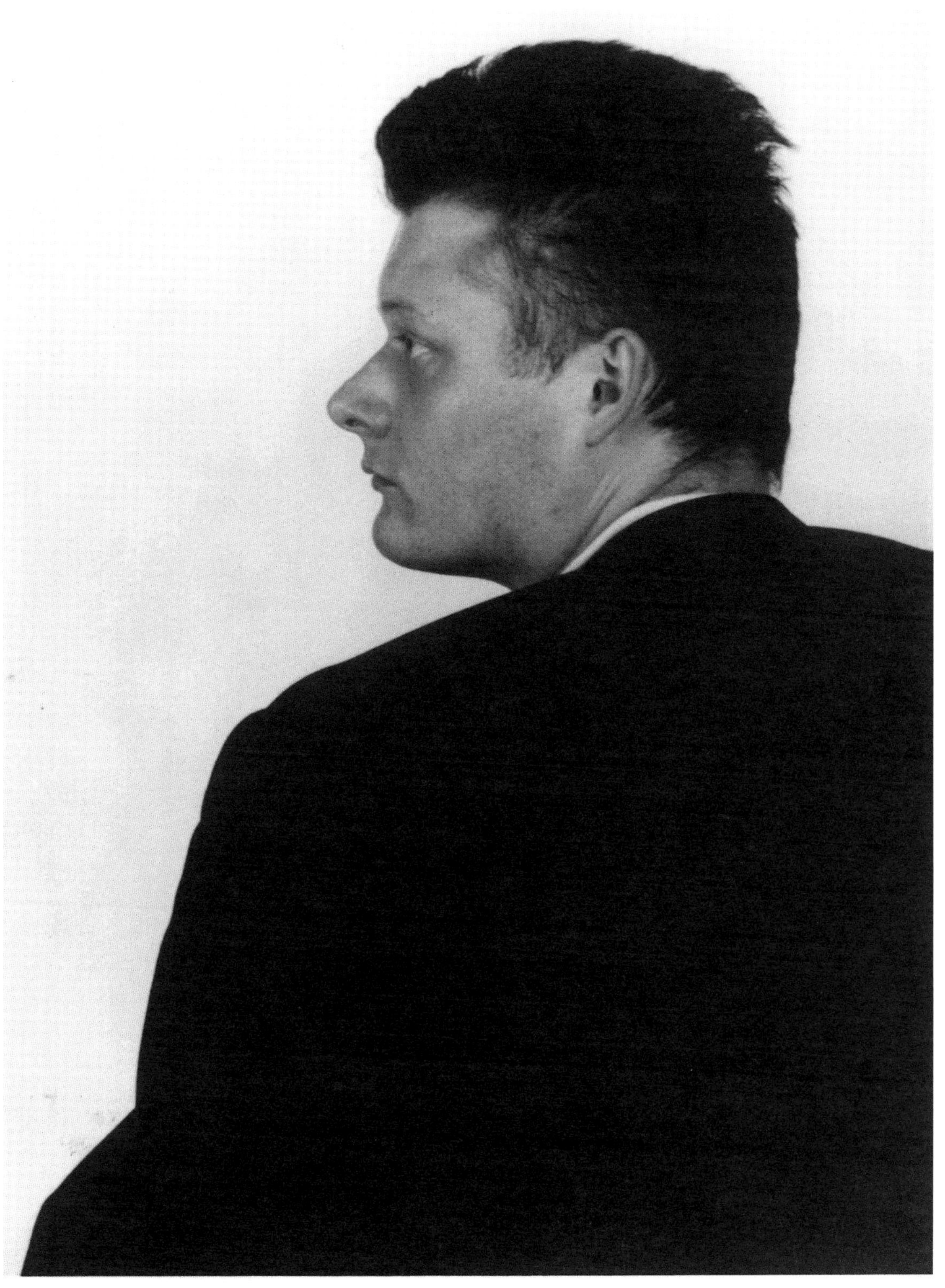

Thomas Ruff *Portrait* 1986 color photograph mounted on Plexiglas 85 3/4 x 70 in.

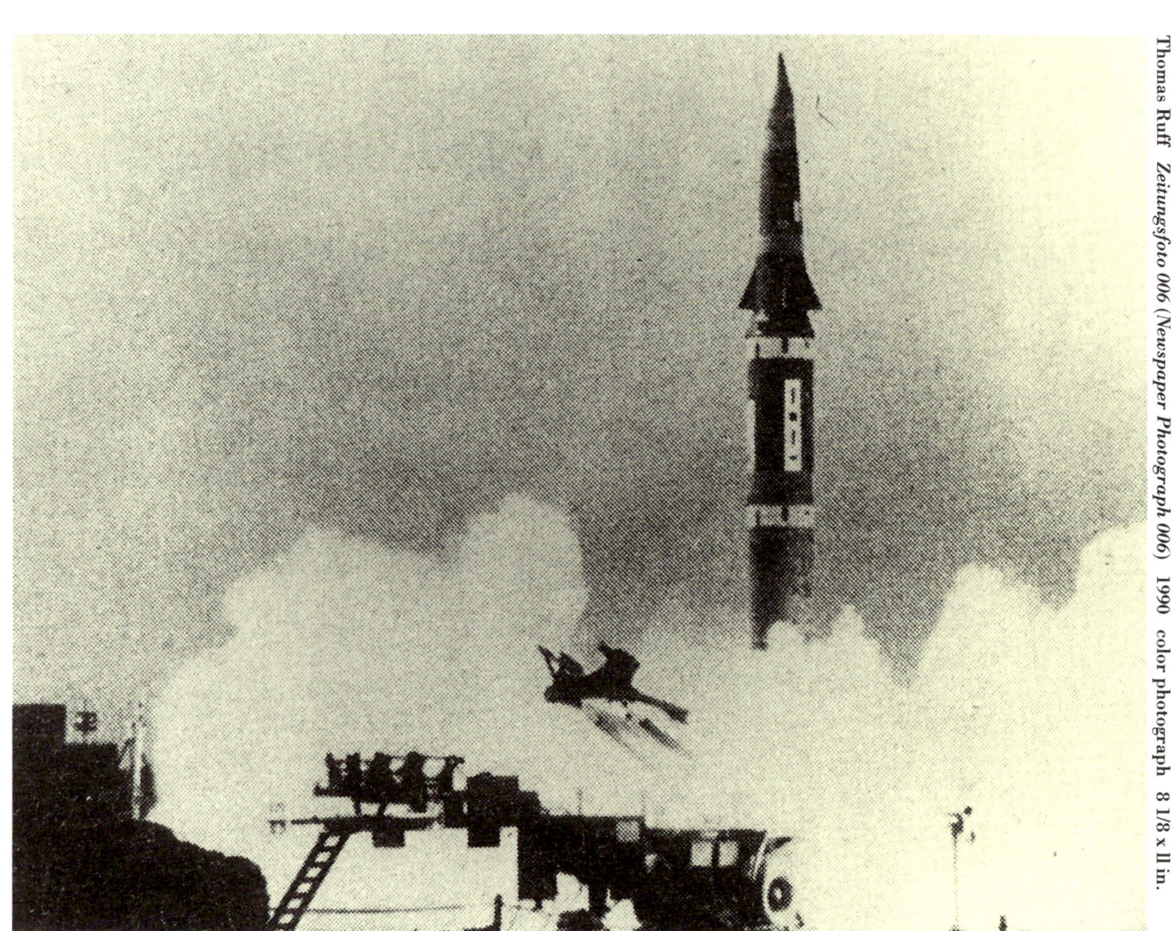

Thomas Ruff *Zeitungsfoto 006 (Newspaper Photograph 006)* 1990 color photograph 8 1/8 x 11 in.

LOTHAR BAUMGARTEN

Born 1944, Rheinsberg, Germany
Studied at Staatliche Kunstakademie, Düsseldorf
Lives and works in Düsseldorf

BIBLIOGRAPHY

Avgikos, Jan. "Anthropological War." *Artscribe* 75 (May 1989), pp. 63–65.

Baumgarten, Lothar and M. Opitz. *Té Né Té*. Düsseldorf, 1974.

—. *Die Namen der Bäume*. Eindhoven: Stedelijk van Abbemuseum, 1982.

—. *Land of the Spotted Eagle*. Mönchengladbach: Museum Abteiberg, 1983.

—. *Señores Naturales*. Venice: 41st Biennale, 1984.

—. *Tierra de los Perros Mudos*. Amsterdam: Stedelijk Museum, 1985.

—. *Accès aux quais (Tableaux Parisiens)*. Paris: ARC/Musée d'Art Moderne, 1986.

—. *Makunaíma*. New York: Marian Goodman Gallery, 1987.

—. "A Project for Artforum." *Artforum* 26, no. 7 (March 1988), pp. 108–111.

—. *Carbon*. New York: Marian Goodman Gallery, 1991.

*Cooke, Lynne and Mark Francis. *Carnegie International 1991*. exh. cat. Pittsburgh: Carnegie Museum of Art, 1991, vol 1.

Gale, Peggy. "Lothar Baumgarten's 'The Origin of the Night.'" *Parachute* 43 (June–August 1986), pp. 5–9.

Johnson, Ken. "Orinoco Defense." *Art in America* 76, no. 10 (October 1988), pp. 184–191.

Owens, Craig. "Improper Names." *Art in America* 74, no. 10 (October 1986), pp. 126–135.

Rorimer, Anne. "Lothar Baumgarten in Pittsburgh: The Tongue of the Cherokee." *Parachute* 58 (Spring 1990), pp. 4–9.

* Publication with up-to-date biography and bibliography.

Bernd Becher
Born 1931, Siegen, Germany
Studied at Staatliche Akademie der Bildenden Künste, Stuttgart; and Staatliche Kunstakademie, Düsseldorf

Hilla Becher
Born 1934, Potsdam, Germany
Studied at Staatliche Kunstakademie, Düsseldorf

Live and work in Düsseldorf

BIBLIOGRAPHY

Andre, Carl. "A Note on Bernhard and Hilla Becher." *Artforum* 11, no. 4 (December 1972), pp. 59–61.

Aus der Distanz: Photographien von Bernd und Hilla Becher, Andreas Gursky, Candida Höfer, Axel Hütte, Thomas Ruff, Thomas Struth, Petra Wunderlich. exh. cat. Düsseldorf: Kunstsammlung Nordrhein-Westfalen, 1991 (German).

Becher, Bernhard (Bernd) and Hilla. *Anonyme Skulpturen: Eine Typologie technischer Bauten*. Düsseldorf: Art Press Verlag, 1970 (German).

——. *Framework Houses from the Siegen Industrial Area*. Munich: Schirmer/Mosel Verlag, 1977.

——. *Fördertürme, Chevalements, Mineheads*. Munich: Schirmer/Mosel Verlag, 1985 (German, French, English).

——. *Water Towers* Cambridge, Mass.: MIT Press, 1988.

——. *Blast Furnaces*. Cambridge, Mass.: MIT Press, 1990.

——. *Pennsylvania Coal Mine Tipples*. New York: Dia Center for the Arts and Munich: Schirmer/Mosel Verlag, 1991.

Bernd and Hilla Becher. exh. cat. La Jolla, Calif.: La Jolla Museum of Contemporary Art, 1974.

Bernd and Hilla Becher. exh. cat. Eindhoven: Stedelijk van Abbemuseum, 1981.

Bernd and Hilla Becher: Tipologie, Typologien, Typologies. exh. cat. Venice: 44th Biennale, 1990 (Italian, German, English).

Grauerholz, A. and Anne Ramsden. "Photographing Industrial Architecture: An Interview with Hilla and Bernd Becher." *Parachute* 22 (Spring 1981), pp. 14–19.

JOSEPH BEUYS

Born 1921, Krefeld, Germany
Died 1986, Düsseldorf, Germany
Studied at Staatliche Kunstakademie, Düsseldorf
Lived and worked in Düsseldorf

BIBLIOGRAPHY

Adriani, Götz et al. *Joseph Beuys — Life and Works*. Woodbury, N. Y.: Barron's, 1979.

Bastian, Heiner, ed. *Joseph Beuys: Skulpturen und Objekte*. exh. cat. Berlin: Martin-Gropius-Bau and Munich: Schirmer/Mosel Verlag, 1988 (German).

Buchloh, Benjamin H. D., Rosalind Krauss, and Annette Michelson. "Joseph Beuys at the Guggenheim." *October* 12 (Spring 1980), pp. 3–21.

Energy Plan for the Western Man: Joseph Beuys in America. Writings and Interviews with the Artist. Compiled by Carin Kuoni. New York: Four Walls Eight Windows, 1990.

Joseph Beuys: Ideas and Actions. exh. cat. New York: Hirschl and Adler Modern, 1988.

Kuspit, Donald. "Beuys: Fat, Felt, and Alchemy." *Art in America* 68, no. 5 (May 1980), pp. 78–89.

McEvilley, Thomas. "Hic Jacet Beuys." *Artforum* 24, no. 9 (May 1986), pp. 130–131.

Schellmann, Jörg, ed. *Joseph Beuys: Multiples*. 6th edn. Munich and New York: Edition Schellmann, 1985 (German, English).

Sharp, Willoughby. "An Interview with Joseph Beuys." *Artforum* 8, no. 4 (December 1969), pp. 40–47.

*Stachelhausen, Heiner. *Joseph Beuys*. Trans. David Britt. New York: Abbeville Press, 1991.

Tisdall, Caroline. *Joseph Beuys*. exh cat. Solomon R. Guggenheim Museum, New York, 1979.

Zweite, Armin. *Joseph Beuys: Natur, Materie, Form*. exh. cat. Düsseldorf: Kunstsammlung Nordrhein-Westfalen, 1991 (German).

* Publication with up-to-date biography and bibliography.

Bernhard Blume
Born 1937, Dortmund, Germany

Studied at Staatliche Kunstakademie, Düsseldorf; Hochschule für Bildende Künste, Düsseldorf; and Universität zu Köln, Cologne

Anna Blume
Born 1937, Bork, Germany

Studied at Staatliche Kunstakademie, Düsseldorf

Live and work in Cologne

BIBLIOGRAPHY

Anna und Bernhard Blume: Gegenseitig. exh. cat. Bonn: Galerie Philomene Magers and Cologne: Balloni Verlag, 1990 (German).

Behind the Eyes: Eight German Artists. exh cat. San Francisco Museum of Modern Art, 1986.

Bernhard Johannes Blume: Fotoarbeiten, 1970–1984. exh. cat. Bonn: Rheinisches Landesmuseum, 1989 (German).

Blume, Anna and Bernhard. "Im Wald: A Project for Artforum." *Artforum* 30, no. 3 (November 1991), pp. 126–127.

Hentschel, Martin. "Bernhard Johannes Blume: Galerie Philomene Magers." *Artforum* 25, no. 8 (April 1987), p. 142.

Kurzner, Lisa. *Projects: Bernhard and Anna Blume*. exh. brochure. New York: Museum of Modern Art, 1989.

Vanishing Presence. exh cat. Minneapolis: Walker Art Center and New York: Rizzoli, 1989.

*Weibel, Peter. *Anna und Bernhard Blume: Vasen-Extasen*. Frankfurt: Museum für Moderne Kunst, 1991 (German).

Weiss, Evelyn. "Bernhard Johannes Blume: 'Magischer Determinismus.'" *Kunstforum International* 18 (1976), pp. 188–205 (German).

Born 1941, Munich, Germany
Lives and works in Hamburg-Harburg

BIBLIOGRAPHY

Borday, Jean-Pierre. "Hanne Darboven or the Dimension of Time and Culture." *Parkett* 10 (1986), pp. 104–111.

Graw, Isabelle. "Marking Time: Time and Writing in the Work of Hanne Darboven." *Artscribe*, no. 79 (January–February 1990), pp. 68–71.

**Hanne Darboven: Primitive Zeit/Uhrzeit: Primitive Time/Clock Time*. Philadelphia: Goldie Paley Gallery, Moore College of Art and Design, 1990.

Hanne Darboven: Für Rainer Werner Fassbinder. exh cat. Munich: Kunstraum, 1989 (German).

Kuspit, Donald. "System as Desire: Hanne Darboven." *Art in America* 68, nos. 6–8 (Summer 1980), pp. 118–119.

Lippard, Lucy. "Deep in Numbers." *Artforum* 12, no. 2 (October 1973), pp. 35–39.

Pohlen, Annelie. "Hanne Darboven's Time: The Content of Consciousness." *Artforum* 21, no. 8 (April 1983), pp. 52–53.

Van Bruggen, Coosje. "*Today* Crossed Out, an Introduction by Coosje van Bruggen to *Today*, a Project by Hanne Darboven." *Artforum* 26, no. 5 (January 1988), pp. 70–73.

* Publication with up-to-date biography and bibliography.

HANS-PETER FELDMANN

Born 1941, Düsseldorf, Germany
Lives and works in Düsseldorf

BIBLIOGRAPHY

Feldmann, Hans-Peter. *Eine Firma*. Munich and Berlin: Siemens AG, 1991.

"Hans-Peter Feldmann." *Flash Art* 52–53 (February–March 1975), p. 26.

Lippert, Walter. "Das Sammlerporträt Hans-Peter Feldmann." *Kunstforum* 19 (January 1977), pp. 38–47 (German).

—.**Hans-Peter Feldmann/Das Museum im Kopf*. Cologne: Verlag der Buchhandlung Walther König, 1989 (German).

Messler, Norbert. "Ein 'Bild' von Feldmann." *Wolkenkratzer Art Journal* 3 (May–June 1988), pp. 26–31 (German).

Metzger, Rainer. "Hans-Peter Feldmann." *Flash Art* 24 (April 1991), p. 148.

Schmalen, Norbert. *Hans-Peter Feldmann: Arbeiten*. exh cat. Kunstverein Region Heinsberg, 1991 (German).

Schmid, Joachim. "Werner Lippert: Hans-Peter Feldmann/Das Museum im Kopf." *European Photography* 46 (April–June 1991), pp. 42–43.

Born 1952, Füssen, Germany
Studied at Akademie der Bildenden Künste, Munich
Lives and works in Areuse, Switzerland

BIBLIOGRAPHY

Dietrich, Dorothea. "An Interview with Günther Förg." *Print Collector's Newsletter* 20, no. 3 (July–August 1989), pp. 81–84.

Günther Förg. exh. cat. Newport Beach, Calif.: Newport Harbor Art Museum, 1989.

Günther Förg. exh. cat. Stuttgart: Edition Cantz, 1990 (German, English).

**Günther Förg.* exh. cat. Musée d'Art Moderne de la Vılle de Paris, 1991 (French, English).

Kuspit, Donald. "Totalitarian Space: The Installations of Günther Förg and Gerhard Merz." *Arts Magazine* 63, no. 10 (Summer 1989), pp. 44–50.

Parkett 26 (1990), issue on Günther Förg. Articles by John Caldwell, Wılfried Dickhoff, and Catherine Queloz (German, English).

Schenker, Christoph. "Günther Förg: An Effort to Re-Engage the Rubble of Modernism — an Incomplete, Liquidated Project — and to Render It Useful through Fresh Conclusions." *Flash Art* 144 (January–February 1989), pp. 66–70.

Schmidt-Wulffen. "Günther Förg Interview: When I'm Uninspired I Go to the Cinema to See a Godard." *Flash Art* 144 (January–February, 1989), pp. 71, 118.

Un'altra obiettività/Another Objectivity. exh. cat. Paris: Centre National des Arts Plastiques; Prato, Italy: Museo d'Arte Contemporanea Luigi Pecci; and Milan: Idea Books, 1989 (Italian, English).

* Publication with up-to-date biography and bibliography.

ANSELM KIEFER

Born 1945, Donaueschingen, Germany
Studied at Universität Freiburg; Staatliche Akademie der Bildenden Künste, Karlsruhe; and Staatliche Kunstakademie, Düsseldorf
Lives and works in Buchen im Odenwald

BIBLIOGRAPHY

*Adriani, Götz, ed. *The Books of Anselm Kiefer, 1969–1990.* Trans. Bruni Mayor. New York: George Braziller, 1991.

Anselm Kiefer: Bruch und Einung. exh. cat. New York: Marian Goodman Gallery, 1987.

Anselm Kiefer. exh. cat. Nationalgalerie Berlin, 1991 (German).

Dietrich, Dorothea. "Anselm Kiefer's 'Johannisnacht II': A Text Book." *Print Collector's Newsletter* 15, no. 2 (May–June 1984), pp. 41–44.

Haxthausen, Charles W. "Kiefer in America: Reflections on a Retrospective." *Kunstchronik* (January 1989), pp. 1–16.

Huyssen, Andreas, "Anselm Kiefer: The Terror of History, the Temptation of Myth." *October* 48 (Spring 1989), pp. 25–45.

Kuspit, Donald B. "The Night Mind." *Artforum* 21, no. 1 (September 1982), pp. 64–67.

Madoff, Steven Henry. "Anselm Kiefer: A Call to Memory." *Art News* 86, no. 8 (October 1987), pp. 125–130.

Rosenthal, Mark. *Anselm Kiefer.* exh. cat. Philadelphia Museum of Art and Art Institute of Chicago, 1987.

MARTIN KIPPENBERGER

Born 1953, Dortmund, Germany
Studied at Hochschule für Bildende Künste, Hamburg
Lives and works in Cologne

BIBLIOGRAPHY

Das Medium der Fotografie ist berechtigt, Denkanstösse zu geben: Sammlung F. C. Gundlach. exh. cat. Kunstverein Hamburg, 1989 (German, English).

Ellis, Stephen. "The Boys in the Bande." *Art in America* 76, no. 12 (December 1988), pp. 110–125, 167–169.

Koether, Jutta. "Who Is Martin Kippenberger and Why Are They Saying Such Terrible Things about Him?" *Artscribe* 73 (January–February 1989), pp. 52–57.

——. "Martin Kippenberger" (interview). *Flash Art* 156 (January–February 1991), pp. 88–93.

* *Martin Kippenberger: I Had a Vision*. exh. cat. San Francisco Museum of Modern Art, 1991.

Martin Kippenberger: Heavy Mädel. exh. cat. New York: Pace/MacGill Gallery and Cologne: Galerie Gisela Capitain, 1991.

Martin Kippenberger: Heavy Burschi. exh. cat. Cologne: Kölnischer Kunstverein, 1991 (German).

Parkett 19 (1989), issue on Martin Kippenberger. Articles by Bice Curiger, Diedrich Diedrichsen, Patrick Frey, and Martin Prinzhorn.

Riemschneider, Burkhard. *Martin Kippenberger: Ten Years After*. Cologne: Benedikt Taschen Verlag, 1991 (German, English, French).

* Publication with up-to-date biography and bibliography.

ASTRID KLEIN

Born 1951, Cologne, Germany
Studied at Fachhochschule für Kunst und Design, Cologne
Lives and works in Cologne

BIBLIOGRAPHY

* *Astrid Klein: Photoworks, 1984–1989*. exh. cat. Hanover: Kestner-Gesellschaft; London: Institute of Contemporary Arts; Vienna: Wiener Secession; and Graz: Forum Stadtpark, 1989.

Blanchette, Manon and Wolfgang Max Faust. *Blickpunkte*. exh. cat. Montreal: Musée d'Art Contemporain, 1989 (French, English).

Dault, Gary Michael. "Savage Glyphs." *C Magazine* 16 (December 1987), pp. 22–23.

Flusser, Vilem. "Astrid Klein—Das Entsetzen." *European Photography* 9 (April–June 1988), pp. 36–38.

Grüterich, Marlies. "Natural Emotions for Artificial Worlds." *Parachute* 5 (Winter 1981), pp. 20–23.

Memory and Vision: Astrid Klein and Katharina Sieverding. exh. brochure. San Francisco: Artspace, 1988.

Ottmann, Klaus. *Astrid Klein*. exh. brochure. Middletown, Conn.: Center for the Arts, Wesleyan University, 1991.

Philippi, Desa. "Cerebral Somersault: Astrid Klein." *Artscribe*, no. 65 (September–October 1987), pp. 38–40.

Reste des Authentischen: Deutsche Fotobilder der 80er Jahre/German Photographic Images of the 80's. exh. cat. Essen: Museum Folkwang, 1986 (German, English).

Born 1940, Dessau, Germany
Studied at Staatliche Kunstakademie, Düsseldorf
Lives and works in Düsseldorf

BIBLIOGRAPHY

* Blanchette, Manon and Wolfgang Max Faust. *Blickpunkte.* exh. cat. Montreal: Musée d'Art Contemporain, 1989 (French, English).

Imi Knoebel: Ausstellungsinstallationen, 1968–1988. exh. cat. Maastrict: Bonnefantenmuseum, 1989 (German).

Imi Knoebel. exh. cat. New York: Dia Art Foundation, 1988.

Imi Knoebel. exh. cat. Winterthur: Kunstmuseum and Bonn: Städtisches Kunstmuseum, 1983 (German).

Kuspit, Donald. "Imi Knoebel's Triangle." *Artforum* 25, no. 5 (January 1987), pp. 72–79.

Schenker, Christoph. "Imi Knoebel." *Flash Art* 24, no. 161 (November–December 1991), pp. 103–107.

Storr, Robert. "Beuys's Boys." *Art in America* 76 (March 1988), pp. 96–103.

Wechsler, Max. "Imi Knoebel: Das Vermessen der Empfindung/The Surveyal of Sensations." *Parkett* 17 (1988), pp. 6–11, 14–21 (German, English).

* Publication with up-to-date biography and bibliography.

REINHARD MUCHA

Born 1950, Düsseldorf, Germany
Studied at Staatliche Kunstakademie, Düsseldorf
Lives and works in Düsseldorf

BIBLIOGRAPHY

Celant, Germano. "Stations on a Journey." *Artforum* 24, no. 4 (December 1985), pp. 76–79.

Cooke, Lynne. "Reinhard Mucha." *Artscribe* 62 (March–April), pp. 56–88.

—. and Mark Francis. *Carnegie International 1991.* exh. cat. Pittsburgh: Carnegie Museum of Art, 1991, vol. 1.

Frey, Patrick. "Reinhard Mucha: Connections." *Parkett* 12 (March 1987), pp. 113–119.

* Halbreich, Kathy. *Culture and Commentary: An Eighties Perspective.* exh. cat. Washington, D.C.: Hirshhorn Museum and Sculpture Garden, 1990.

Monk, Philip. "Reinhard Mucha: The Silence of Presentation," *Parachute* 51 (June–August 1988), pp. 22–28.

Mucha, Reinhard. "A Project for Artforum by Reinhard Mucha." *Artforum* 26, no. 2 (October 1987), pp. 96–99.

Schenker, Christoph. "Reinhard Mucha." *Flash Art* 135 (Summer 1987), pp. 89–91.

SIGMAR POLKE

Born 1944, Oels, Silesia (now Olesnica, Poland)
Studied at Staatliche Kunstakademie, Düsseldorf
Lives and works in Cologne

BIBLIOGRAPHY

Baker, Kenneth. "Addition + Abundance: Sigmar Polke." *Artforum* 29, no. 8 (April 1991), pp. 82–88.

Frailey, Stephen. "Sigmar Polke: Photographic Obstruction." *Print Collector's Newsletter* 26, no. 3 (July–August 1985), pp. 77–80.

Gintz, Claude. "Polke's Slow Dissolve." *Art in America* 73, no. 12 (December 1985), pp. 102–109.

Paoletti, John T. "Higher Beings Command: The Prints of Sigmar Polke." *Print Collector's Newsletter* 22, no. 2 (May–June 1991), pp. 37–44.

Parkett 30 (1991), issue on Sigmar Polke. Articles by Bice Curiger, Roger Denson, Gary Garrels, Laszlo Glozer, Dave Hickey, Thomas McEvilley, Kevin Power, and Gabrielle Wix (German, English).

"Poison Is Effective; Painting Is Not. Bice Curiger in Conversation with Sigmar Polke, December 18, 1984," *Parkett* 26 (1990), pp. 18–26.

Poetter, Jochen, Sigmar Polke: Fotografien. exh. cat. Kunsthalle Baden-Baden and Stuttgart: Edition Cantz, 1990 (German, English).

* *Sigmar Polke.* exh. cat. San Francisco Museum of Modern Art, 1990.

* Publication with up-to-date biography and bibliography.

BERNHARD PRINZ

Born 1953, Fürth, Germany
Studied at Academy of Fine Arts, Nuremberg
Lives and works in Hamburg

BIBLIOGRAPHY

Bernhard Prinz. exh. cat. London: Serpentine Gallery, 1988.

* *Bernhard Prinz: Idee-Ideal-Ideologie.* exh. cat. Nuremberg: Kunsthalle, 1989 (German).

Cooke, Lynne. "Dread and Desire." *Art International* 5 (1988), p. 75.

Das Medium der Fotografie ist berechtigt, Denkanstösse zu geben: Sammlung F. C. Gundlach. exh. cat. Kunstverein Hamburg, 1989 (German, English).

Metzger, Rainer. "Bernhard Prinz." *Flash Art* 145 (March–April 1989), pp. 118–119.

Schmidt-Wulffen, Stephan. "Bernhard Prinz." *Noema* 12/13 (1987), p. 120 (German).

—. "Bernhard Prinz." *documenta 8.* exh. cat. Kassel: Weber and Weidemeyer, 1987, vol. 2, pp. 196–197 (German).

Von Drateln, Doris. "Bernhard Prinz, Monographie." *Kunstforum International*, no. 108 (June–July 1990), pp. 160–183 (German).

Born 1932, Dresden, Germany
Studied at Kunstakademie Dresden; and Staatliche Kunstakademie, Düsseldorf
Lives and works in Cologne

BIBLIOGRAPHY

Buchloh, Benjamin H. D. "A Note on Gerhard Richter's *October 18, 1977*." *October* 48 (Spring 1989), pp. 89–109.

Dietrich, Dorothea. "Gerhard Richter: An Interview." *Print Collector's Newsletter* 16, no. 4 (September–October 1985), pp. 128–132.

Ellis, Stephen. "The Elusive Gerhard Richter." *Art in America* 74, no. 11 (November 1986), pp. 130–139, 186.

Gerhard Richter Paintings. exh. cat. Chicago: Museum of Contemporary Art and Toronto: Art Gallery of Ontario, 1988.

Gerhard Richter 1988/89. exh. cat. Rotterdam: Museum Boymans-van Beuningen, 1989 (Dutch, English).

Gerhard Richter: Mirrors. exh. cat. London: Anthony d'Offay Gallery, 1991.

Paoletti, John T. "Gerhard Richter: Ambiguity as an Agent of Awareness." *Print Collector's Newsletter* 19, no. 1 (March–April 1988), pp. 1–6.

Rainbird, Sean, Stefan Germer, and Neal Ascherson. *Gerhard Richter*. exh. cat. London: Tate Gallery, 1991.

Van Bruggen, Coosje. "Gerhard Richter: Painting as a Moral Act." *Artforum* 23, no. 9 (May 1985), pp. 82–91.

Zweite, Armin. *Atlas*. Munich: Städtische Galerie im Lenbachhaus and Verlag Fred Jahn, 1989 (German).

PETER ROEHR

Born 1944, Lauenburg, Pomerania (now Lebork, Poland)
Studied at Werkkunstschule, Wiesbaden
Died 1968, Frankfurt, Germany

BIBLIOGRAPHY

Fuchs, Rudi H., et al. *Peter Roehr*. Trans. James K. Whitman. Cologne: DuMont, 1977 (German, English).

* Lippert, Werner and Paul Maenz. *Peter Roehr*. Gerd de Vries, ed. Frankfurt am Main: Museum für Moderne Kunst, 1991 (German, English).

Messler, Norbert. "Peter Roehr." *Artforum* 27, no. 6 (February 1989), pp. 144–145.

—. "Peter Roehr." *Noema* 21 (November–December 1988), pp. 46–51 (German).

Peter Roehr: Zum 20. Todestag, 1968–1988. exh. cat. Cologne: Galerie Paul Maenz, 1988 (German, English).

THOMAS RUFF

Born 1958, Zell am Harmersbach, Germany
Studied at Staatliche Kunstakademie, Düsseldorf
Lives and works in Düsseldorf

BIBLIOGRAPHY

Aus der Distanz: Photografien von Bernd und Hilla Becher, Andreas Gursky, Candida Höfer, Axel Hütte, Thomas Ruff, Thomas Struth, Petra Wunderlich. exh. cat. Düsseldorf: Kunstsammlung Nordrhein-Westfalen, 1991 (German).

Harten, Jürgen and David A. Ross. *BiNationale: German Art of the Late 80's.* exh. cat. Düsseldorf: Städtische Kunsthalle, Kunstsammlung Nordrhein-Westfalen and Kunstverein für die Rheinlande und Westfalen; and Boston: Institute of Contemporary Art and Museum of Fine Arts, 1988 (German, English).

Humeltenberg, Hanna. "The Magic Realism in Thomas Ruff's Pictures." *Parkett* 19 (1989), pp. 16–27.

Parkett 28 (1991), issue on Thomas Ruff. Articles by Norman Bryson, Trevor Fairbrother, Marc Freidus, and Jörg Johnen.

Pohlen, Annelie. "Deep Surface." *Artforum* 29, no. 8 (April 1991), pp. 114–118.

Rubenstein, Meyer Raphael. "Apollo in Düsseldorf: The Photographs of Thomas Ruff." *Arts Magazine* 63, no. 2 (October 1988), pp. 41–43.

Ruff, Thomas. "Houses by Thomas Ruff." *Artforum* 27, no. 7 (March 1989), pp. 102–105. Portfolio with note by Ida Panicelli.

Thomas Ruff. exh. cat. Bonn: Bonner Kunstverein, 1991 (German).

Thomas Ruff: Portraits, Houses, Stars. exh. cat. Amsterdam: Stedelijk Museum, 1989 (Dutch, German, French).

Thomas Ruff: Portraits. exh. cat. Velbert: Museum Schloss Hardenburg and Frankfurt am Main: Portikus, 1988 (German).

* *Typologies: Nine Contemporary Photographers.* exh. cat. Newport Beach, Calif.: Newport Harbor Art Museum, 1991.

* Publication with up-to-date biography and bibliography.

KATHARINA SIEVERDING

Born 1944, Prague, Czechoslovakia
Studied at Staatliche Kunstakademie, Düsseldorf
Lives and works in Düsseldorf

BIBLIOGRAPHY

Individuelle Positionen. exh. cat. Cologne: Josef-Haubrich Kunsthalle, 1990 (German).

Katharina Sieverding: Bilder aus den Zyklen XXVIII-XI, 1987–1978. exh. cat. Karlsruhe: Badischer Kunstverein and Kassel: Kasseler Kunstverein, 1987 (German).

Katharina Sieverding. exh. cat. Munich: Galerie Barbara Gross, 1990 (German).

Katharina Sieverding. exh. cat. Düsseldorf: Stadt-Sparkasse, 1988. Text by Jürgen Harten (German).

Katharina Sieverding: Grossfotos I-X/75-77. exh. cat. Essen: Museum Folkwang, 1977 (German).

Katharina Sieverding: Norad XVIII-XXVIII, 1980. exh. cat. Darmstadt: Mathildenhöhe, 1983 (German).

L'occhio dell'artista, L'occhio della camera/Das Auge des Kunstlers, Das Auge der Kamera. exh. cat. Frankfurt am Main: Frankfurter Kunstverein and Ravenna: Pinacoteca, 1986 (Italian, German).

Medium Fotographie. exh. cat. Oldenburg: Oldenburger Kunstverein and Hamburg: PPS Galerie, 1985 (German).

Memory and Vision: Astrid Klein and Katharina Sieverding. exh. brochure. San Francisco: Artspace, 1988.

Self-Portrait. exh. cat. Tokyo: Metropolitan Museum of Photography, 1991 (Japanese, English).

Zur Sache Selbst: Künstlerinnen des 20. Jahrhunderts. exh. cat. Museum Wiesbaden, 1990 (German).

THOMAS STRUTH

Born 1954, Geldern, Germany
Studied at Staatliche Kunstakademie, Düsseldorf
Lives and works in Düsseldorf

BIBLIOGRAPHY

Aus der Distanz: Photografien von Bernd und Hilla Becher, Andreas Gursky, Candida Höfer, Axel Hütte, Thomas Ruff, Thomas Struth, Petra Wunderlich. exh. cat. Düsseldorf: Kunstsammlung Nordrhein-Westfalen, 1991 (German).

Decter, Joshua. "Thomas Struth—Marian Goodman Gallery." *Artscribe International* 85 (January–February 1991), pp. 80–81.

A Dialogue about Recent American and European Photography. exh. cat. Museum of Contemporary Art, Los Angeles, 1991.

Hapgood, Susan. "Thomas Struth at Marian Goodman Gallery." *Art in America* 79, no. 1 (January 1991), pp. 125–126.

Kuspit, Donald. "Thomas Struth—Marian Goodman." *Artforum* 29, no. 4 (December 1990), pp. 132–133.

Loock, Ulrich. "Thomas Struth." *Creative Camera* 5 (May 1988), pp. 14–19.

—. "Unbewusste Orte/Unconscious Places." *Parkett* 23 (March 1990), pp. 21–31 (German, English).

Portraits—Thomas Struth. exh. cat. New York: Marian Goodman Gallery, 1990.

Schwabsky, Barry. "Thomas Struth." *Arts Magazine* 65, no. 4 (December 1990), p. 83.

Thomas Struth—Photographs. exh. cat. Renaissance Society at the University of Chicago, 1990.

* *Typologies: Nine Contemporary Photographers*. exh. cat. Newport Beach, Calif.: Newport Harbor Art Museum, 1991.

Un'altra obiettività/Another Objectivity. exh. cat. Paris: Centre Nationale des Arts Plastiques; Prato, Italy: Museo d'Arte Contemporanea Luigi Pecci; and Milan: Idea Books, 1989 (Italian, English).

* Publication with up-to-date biography and bibliography.

SELECTED GENERAL BIBLIOGRAPHY

BOOKS AND EXHIBITION CATALOGUES

Amsterdam-Paris-Düsseldorf. exh. cat. New York: Solomon R. Guggenheim Museum, 1972.

Another Objectivity. exh. cat. London: Institute of Contemporary Arts, 1988.

Aus der Distanz: Photographien von Bernd und Hilla Becher, Andreas Gursky, Candida Höfer, Axel Hütte, Thomas Ruff, Thomas Struth, Petra Wunderlich. exh. cat. Kunstsammlung Nordrhein-Westfalen, 1991 (German).

Avant-Garde Photography in Germany, 1919–1939. exh. cat. San Francisco Museum of Modern Art, 1980.

Behind the Eyes: Eight German Artists. exh. cat. San Francisco Museum of Modern Art, 1986.

La Biennale di Venezia: Section of Visual Arts. exh. cat. 39th Biennale, Venice, 1980.

Blanchette, Manon and Wolfgang Max Faust. *Blickpunkte.* exh. cat. Montreal: Musée d'Art Contemporain, 1989 (French, English).

Chevrier, Jean-François. *Photo-Kunst: Arbeiten aus 150 Jahren/Du XXème au XIXème siècle, aller et retour.* exh. cat. Graphische Sammlung Staatsgalerie Stuttgart, 1989 (German).

Coke, Van Deren. *Avant-Garde Photography in Germany, 1919–1939.* New York: Pantheon, 1982.

A Dialogue about Recent American and European Photography. exh. cat. Museum of Contemporary Art, Los Angeles, 1991.

Dickhoff, Wilfried, Wilhelm Schürmann, and Monika Sprüth, *Das Licht von der Anderen Seite: Photographie.* exh. cat. Cologne: Galerie Monika Sprüth and Hamburg: PPS Galerie and F.C. Gundlach, 1988 (German).

documenta 6, Band 2: Fotografie, Film, Video. exh. cat. Kassel, 1977 (German).

Das Foto als autonomes Bild: Experimentelle Gestaltung, 1839–1989. exh. cat. Kunsthalle Bielefeld, 1989 (German).

German Photography: Documentation and Introspection. exh. cat. Ridgefield, Conn.: Aldrich Museum of Contemporary Art, 1990.

Grasskamp, Walter. *Der vergessliche Engel: Künstlerportraits für Fortgeschrittene.* Munich: Silke Schreiber, 1986 (German).

Grundberg, Andy and Kathleen McCarthy Gauss. *Photography and Art: Interactions since 1946.* exh. cat. Los Angeles County Museum of Art, 1987.

F. C. Gundlach, ed. *Kölner Künstler Photographieren*. Cologne: Verlag der Buchhandlung Walther König, 1988 (German).

Harten, Jürgen and David A. Ross. *BiNationale: German Art of the Late 80's*. exh. cat. Düsseldorf: Städtische Kunsthalle, Kunstsammlung Nordrhein-Westfalen, and Kunstverein für die Rheinlande und Westfalen; and Boston: Institute of Contemporary Art and Museum of Fine Arts, 1988 (German, English).

Krauss, Rolf, Manfred Schmalriede, and Michael Schwarz. *Kunst mit Photographie*. exh. cat. Nationalgalerie Berlin, 1983 (German).

Künstler verwenden Fotografie — heute. exh. cat. Stuttgart: Institute für Auslandsbeziehungen, 1982 (German, English).

Künstlerische Techniken IV: Die Fotografie. exh. cat. Kunsthalle Bielefeld, 1989 (German).

Das Medium der Fotografie ist berechtigt, Denkanstösse zu geben: Sammlung F. C. Gundlach. exh. cat. Kunstverein Hamburg, 1989 (German, English).

Medium Fotografie: Fotoarbeiten bildender Künstler von 1910 bis 1973. exh. cat. Städtisches Museum Leverkusen, 1973 (German).

Medium Photographie. exh. cat. Oldenburg: Oldenburger Kunstverein and Hamburg: PPS Galerie, 1985 (German).

Medium Photographie: 8 Künstler arbeiten mit Fotos. exh. cat. Kunsthalle zu Kiel, 1982 (German).

Molderings, H. *De la photographie: 17 allemands*. exh. cat. Paris: Goethe Institute, 1980 (French).

Momentbild: Künstlerphotographie. exh. cat. Hanover: Kestner-Gesellschaft, 1982 (German).

Neusüss, Floris M., ed. *Fotografie als Kunst — Kunst als Fotografie*. Cologne: DuMont, 1979 (German, English).

L'occhio dell'artista, L'occhio della camera/Das Auge des Künstlers, Das Auge der Kamera. exh. cat. Frankfurt am Main: Frankfurter Kunstverein and Ravenna: Pinacoteca, 1986 (Italian, German).

Reste des Authentischen: deutsche Fotobilder der 80erJahre/German Photographic Images of the 80's. exh. cat. Essen: Museum Folkwang, 1986 (German, English).

Special Affects: The Photographic Experience in Contemporary Art. Milan: Giancarlo Politi Editore, 1989.

Surgence: La Création photographique contemporaine en Allemagne. exh. cat. Musée de la Ville de Poitiers, 1991 (French, English).

Symposium: Die Photographie in der zeitgenössischen Kunst. Stuttgart: Akademie Schloss Solitude and Edition Cantz, 1990 (German).

Typologies: Nine Contemporary Photographers. exh. cat. Newport Beach, Calif.: Newport Harbor Art Museum, 1991.

Un'altra obiettività/Another Objectivity. exh. cat. Paris: Centre National des Arts Plastiques; Prato, Italy: Museo d'Arte Contemporanea Luigi Pecci; and Milan: Idea Books, 1989 (Italian, English).

Von hier aus: Zwei Monaten neue deutsche Kunst in Düsseldorf. exh. cat. Cologne: DuMont, 1984 (German).

Hier et après/Yesterday and After. exh. cat. Montreal Museum of Fine Arts, 1980 (French, English).

PERIODICALS

"Between Past and Future: New German Photography." *Aperture* 123 (Spring 1991), special issue.

Faust, Wolfgang Max. "Deutsche Kunst, hier, heute." *Kunstforum International* 1 (December 1981–January 1982), pp. 24–40. (German).

Hermes, Manfred. "Repetition, Disguises, Documents: How Photography Has Pervaded Two Decades of Contemporary German Art." *Flash Art* 148 (October 1989), pp. 97–103.

"Inszenierte Fotografie: Materialen — Statements und Zitate." *Kunstforum International* 84 (June–August 1986), pp. 184–197 (German).

Magnani, Gregorio. "Ordering Procedures: Photography in Recent German Art." *Arts Magazine* 64, no. 7 (March 1990), pp. 78–83.

Passel, B. and W. M. Faust. "Worüber zu sprechen ist: ein Florilegium aus Kritiken und Rezensionen zum Zeitschnitt: 30 Deutsche." *Kunstforum International* 47 (December 1981–January 1982), pp. 160–184 (German).

"Die Welt als Vorstellung — die Vorstellung als Welt." *Kunstforum International* 84 (June–August 1986), pp. 72–115 (German).

Wınter, Paul. "Manipulieren, ironisieren, malträtieren: das Foto unter der Hand des Künstlers." *das Kunstwerk* 42, no. 1 (March 1989), pp. 5–62 (German).

REPRODUCTION CREDITS

Listed here are the names of the artists included in the exhibition, followed by the names of those who either took or supplied the reproductions of their work.

Lothar Baumgarten: Courtesy the artist; installation view by Douglas M. Parker, Los Angeles
Bernd and Hilla Becher: Courtesy the artists and Schirmer/Mosel Verlag, Munich
Joseph Beuys: Photos by Glenn Halvorson, Walker Art Center
Bernhard and Anna Blume: Photos by Glenn Halvorson, Walker Art Center
Hanne Darboven: Courtesy Busche Galerie, Cologne
Hans-Peter Feldmann: Courtesy the artist
Günther Förg: Courtesy the artist
Anselm Kiefer: Courtesy Marian Goodman Gallery, New York
Martin Kippenberger: James Franklin, courtesy Luhring Augustine Hetzler Gallery, Los Angeles
Astrid Klein: Courtesy Produzentengalerie, Hamburg
Imi Knoebel: Courtesy the artist; installation view by Tom Rautert
Reinhard Mucha: Courtesy the artist
Sigmar Polke: Courtesy Staatliche Kunsthalle Baden-Baden
Bernhard Prinz: Photos by Hege Mundt, Hamburg, courtesy Produzentengalerie, Hamburg
Gerhard Richter: Installation view by Simone Gaensheimer, Munich, courtesy of Städtische Galerie im Lenbachhaus, Munich. Photos of *Atlas* by Simone Gaensheimer, George Meister, and Jutta Simmersbach, Munich; Friedrich Rosenstiel, Cologne; and Archiv Gerhard Richter, Cologne
Peter Roehr: Archiv Paul Maenz, Cologne
Thomas Ruff: Courtesy the artist
Katharina Sieverding: Photos by Klaus Mettig, Düsseldorf
Thomas Struth: Courtesy the artist

STAFF FOR THE EXHIBITION

Director
Kathy Halbreich

Administrative Director
David M. Galligan

Exhibition Curator
Gary Garrels

Curatorial Intern
Toby Kamps

Design Director
Laurie Haycock Makela

Photographer
Glenn Halvorson

Secretarial Assistance
Henrietta Dwyer

Public Relations and Audience Development Director
John K. Hall

Associate Director, Public Relations
Karen Gysin

Development Director
Katharine DeShaw

Finance Director
Mary Polta

Education Director
Margaret O'Neill-Ligon

Assistant Director, Adult Education
Deborah Karasov

Slide-Tape Producer
Peter Murphy

Building Operations Manager
John Lied

Exhibition Installation Supervisors
Kirk McCall
Sandra Daulton Shaughnessy
Cameron Zebrun

Exhibition Installation Crew
Lynn Amlie
Brian Bartholomay
Susan Lindemann Berg
Richard Broberg
Ben Clemence
David Dick
Phil Docken
David Hartman
Lisa Helminiak
Tom Jenn
Richard Lee
Nathan Otterson
Richard Parnell
David Pelto
Dane Peterson
Bill Ploetz
John Voils
Timothy Willette